RACISM CAN THRIVE IF ONE ALLOWS IT!

Bridging the Gap between Multiple Cultures

Doris Goodman

Copyright © 2024 Doris Goodman
All rights reserved
First Edition

PAGE PUBLISHING
Conneaut Lake, PA

First originally published by Page Publishing 2024

ISBN 979-8-88960-678-9 (pbk)
ISBN 979-8-88960-685-7 (digital)

Printed in the United States of America

Is it possible to initiate change,
What would it cost you?

Racism starts from a seed
The seed of racism becomes fertile through its roots.

—Doris Goodman

DORIS GOODMAN

I'd like to acknowledge and give a special thanks to Amerra Little, my granddaughter, for her diligent support and time in typing my written notes for the entire book *Racism Can Thrive If One Allows It*.

BEING BLACK
by Doris Goodman

Being black or white is not my choice
It is God's choice
Seeing that it is we should all be equal
Being white or black is not your choice
It is God's choice
Being black or white
Is not our choice
It is God's choice
Knowing that we should all be equal
Upon his choice
He toned some of us down and lightened some of us up
Which makes life interesting
And above all full of various blends
What more can one ask for?

The author divulges in her personal lifetime experiences. She shares information about growing up with her parents and siblings. The author touches on how her brother's tragedy changed her life.

The book discloses the history of the past and present. This book will allow the reader to understand the anger, pain, suffering, depression, loneliness, and reality of what transpired in the past and how to move forward in today's world.

The author lists several activists of the past and present. The author emphasizes Al Sharpton's point of view regarding the implementation of new laws put into effect that can bring about change, that can protect the rights of all people, which can help create an equal justice system.

The author believes in today's world we the people can move forward and not allow the past to hinder or interrupt the acceleration of the future. She demonstrates the importance of being persistent throughout the book in all her endeavors. The reader will be exposed to how the author's perseverance played a role in her life and how she was able to find ways to overcome her obstacles.

The author ties in the Vietnam War from start to finish. She comments on Annette Gordon Reed, Jane Bolin, and additional activists throughout the book.

The author believes that love and kindness go a long way. She mirrors often who she is and how the reflection in the mirror made a difference in her life in a positive way resulting in a victorious outcome.

CONTENTS

Prologue ix
Introduction...xi
Acknowledgments xiii
Author: Who Am I? xvii
Autobiography xxi

Chapter 1   Multicultural Experiences Growing Up and Parents' History throughout the South 1
Chapter 2   Racism Tried and Failed in My Neighborhood 3
Chapter 3   Racism Thrives if We Allow It.......................7
Chapter 4   The Kickback on Racism Is Worth Today's Challenge 9
Chapter 5   Racism Existed Minimally in My Neighborhood 13
Chapter 6   Many Activists Fought in the Past for Equality...17
Chapter 7   Diversified Community and Families Sharing Food and Recipes 21
Chapter 8   The Life I Once Knew Brings Tears to My Eyes with What I Know Now 25
Chapter 9   One Memory of the Past Spoiled a Barrel of Many Memories 33

Chapter 10	Excerpts from Morgan Avenue Residents	...37
Chapter 11	Referencing Juneteenth: Annette Gordon-Reed	45
Chapter 12	Learning the History of Jane Bolin	51
Chapter 13	Vietnam War	61
Chapter 14	Loudmouth Al Sharpton	77
Chapter 15	The Adult Awakening in Life's Reality	85
Chapter 16	Book Closing	93
Chapter 17	Wall of Fame	99

PROLOGUE

I would like to take a little time to explain to the reader how I came about writing my book. I did not plan or believe I would be writing a book. I did not think or feel it necessary for me to express myself in a literary format. I believe writing this book was an accident.

As I mentioned, I did not plan to write a book on the subject of racism. When the thought crossed my mind at first, I ignored it. I didn't believe it was possible, especially on the subject of racism; however, when I decided to write this book, I felt I was pressured by a driven force that encouraged me to get down on it and write down my life experiences. As a matter of fact, it seemed and felt like God was in the plan.

What I'm trying to say is that I strongly believe God had to inspire me because I did not think it was possible for me without the help of this higher being in my life. As we do things in life many times, we believe we did whatever it was that needed to be done. I believe not only in God but also that he is responsible for all that we do in life, especially when we can't figure out why we did what we do.

As I express my feelings and tell my story, this pertains solely to me and how I felt God was influencing my life for me to tell my story, although I did not anticipate doing this. In life, there comes a time when we as people have to tell our story. In doing this, my intent is to motivate the reader to access themselves and perhaps write their story one day. Many times, we are influenced by others, and we never believe we can be an influencer as well.

My goal is not only to tell my story but also to explain many events that occurred in my life and to make a mention of the good deeds people did in order to help change the laws and the people in today's world. Finally, I realize I'm only one person and I stand alone, but if people could examine themselves, they, too, could make a change toward continuing to improve themselves throughout life for a better tomorrow.

Relatives Who Experienced the Struggle in the South

INTRODUCTION

I decided to tell my story on how things were for me and my family while growing up for many reasons. I know things change as time goes on, but due to racism, it seems the world is at a standstill.

I listened to what my parents had to say about their lives growing up in Alabama. I recall them saying segregation was big. In 1930, lawyers from the National Association for Advancement of Colored People bring a lawsuit stating that separate was not equal and that all children deserve a quality equal education. It was the lawsuits that were combined into the *Brown vs. Board of Education* Supreme Court case that outlawed segregation in schools in 1954.

Despite the court's decision, it took a while to bring about change. Therefore, learning about the struggles as opposed to experiencing them is what drove me to write about my experience contrary to unfavorable times in the past; this is one reason I decided to share my story. It seems people today are frozen in time, although integration is incorporated throughout the world but is coupled with hatred.

Also, another reason I thought to talk about what my upbringing was like is because no matter what's going on in the world today, I can look back with hope for continued change and be able to feed off my past positive experiences in a community of nothing but love and happiness. In addition, I was aware of racism outside of my community and was knowledgeable enough to know it did not exist in my community, which was made up of multiple ethnic backgrounds.

In summary of my introduction, I get to feel a greater love for the world and for who I am.

Adolph and Leola Smiley, parents of author Doris Goodman

ACKNOWLEDGMENTS

Dedicated to Leola and Adolph Smiley, aunts, uncles, cousins, and friends. This book means to me more than anyone could ever imagine. I thank my parents for providing me with a safe environment and for making my way prosperous throughout the years as they watched me grow. My parents laid the foundation to ensure that my siblings and I were well cared for. We were protected, watched, and loved as children. My parents really put down the foundation so that we could be in an environment that included aunts and uncles, who helped make it safe and conducive for learning.

I know if my parents were alive today, they would be proud to see how I further enhanced my lifestyle as well as helped others grow. My parents would be ecstatic to see myself as a retired professional. A successful teacher, making a difference in the lives of children and adults. My parents would be proud of me, especially knowing they had a lot to do with my outcome as they paved the way early on in my childhood development.

My communication skills have allowed me to work well with others in a businesslike setting. By giving support to community members and friends. Teaching others how to develop their goals and carry them out. I have worked with children and adults for thirty-one years. Moreover, I have offered support to people such as advice, giving a helping hand; one might say this is a way of giving back to the community. I am proud to say to this day I lend a hand whenever needed; whether it be to the church or the community, my passion has always been working with people.

In addition, when I look back to where I grew up in Williamsburg, Brooklyn, I didn't come from a family with money, although my father had a great job. In fact, he furthered his education to get a job as a printer pressman. My siblings and I had many challenges, but one thing I can say, love was the one thing that kept my family focused and engaged with one another.

I owe it all to my mother and father, who mentored and cared for my siblings and me. I had two sisters and two brothers; my siblings are Adolph Junior, Leroy, Christine, and Ruth. Even though we never had material things, never went on trips aside from a couple of visits to our grandmother's home in Alabama, we could all feel the love in the family. We were raised with love, understanding, and hope for a bright future.

Furthermore, I thank God for allowing me to have two beautiful parents, Leola and Adolph Smiley, who helped in every way to help me make a difference in my life and who taught others how to get what they are looking for and make the most out of life.

I have been blessed to be able to reach out to people who need assistance, and they don't know how to ask for help. I have opened my arms and extended myself wherever I recognize a need to help someone or to comfort someone.

I love caring for people if I know they are genuinely in need. It means giving directions, advice, or a few minutes of my time to help someone.

As I recognize who I am and understand my purpose on this earth, it's impossible for me not to be there for mankind. Although I've had an adverse reaction by people because they think I overextend myself. I've experienced people saying I am not God and I can't help everybody; this is true, but if people had respect for others and showed it, life would be better. Where I grew up, family and friends looked out for each other.

Last but not least, my parents, Leola and Adolph, had a strong value system. We had a lot of love and compassion for others even if it cost us problems, whether someone was envious or jealous. My parents taught me to be kind even if others don't understand why I do what I do. I had to tune out what others thought and continue to be myself and do what I love for others.

DORIS GOODMAN

AUTHOR: WHO AM I?

I am a strong black woman who appreciates life and who feels a great need to help others who might be faced with challenges. I have always helped people who were in need of assistance. Many times, I've reached out to help make a difference in life or to be a blessing to someone. It's important to know that lending a hand can allow one to truly understand their makeup or who they are. I'm a people person; when I do what I do, I feel I am fulfilling my God-given purpose in life.

Furthermore, I believe life is designed for people to realize it's important to give, share, and be a blessing to others. Life is temporary, and we as human beings should try to understand that humankind is a representation of many cultures. People must all recognize their purpose in life, and they must be willing to do unto others as they would want someone to do for them. I always look at both sides of the coin; the tables could turn.

Moreover, as an individual, I am a people person with nothing but love in my heart. It takes love, kindness, and compassion to really reach out to others. I thank God daily for creating me to want to help others regardless of their heritage, creed, or color. I know as individuals people are different in more ways than one. I know there is only one me; no one else is like me.

As a humanitarian, people should be concerned with enhancing the welfare of others. As my husband always quotes, "I would go to bat for people in other words, giving or helping to address their needs." I feel this is God's creation and is part of my DNA.

As I go through life, nothing stops me from succeeding; if I get a no, I will continue to pursue the situation until I get a yes. I feel fortunate to be in a situation where I can make a difference in my life as well as others'. I strongly believe God's love is upon me and he is love. Yes, God is love, believe it or not; the love is contagious.

In addition, prior to my retirement, I worked well with people in all departments. As a team player, I listen to the opinions and ideas of various workers. It's important to get along in the work field. I helped create a positive environment, which is vital to be successful. I am saying that life has given me ups and downs, but I am one to spring back. I know it's not always been easy, but I can tell you I never gave up no matter what the situation entailed. The lack of one component such as love can cause one to eventually lose their worldly possessions such as money and success.

In closing, I just want people to know what's love got to do with it? Everything. Love is key; without love, I believe it limits one's success, prosperity, and connection to open future doors. God created us for lending a helping hand to someone, a neighbor, or a friend. Who are we? I don't believe God created people in the world to separate themselves and to act like they are superior to any particular group that is not like them. As human beings, people have rights.

As human beings, we have rights! People should be able to exercise their rights without having to fight for their rights. An animal has rights, and if someone is caught mistreating an animal, they will be punished and held accountable for their actions. There are people who will defend or fight to protect animals who are mistreated. It seems like laws are only written to protect animals.

Although there have been many people, such as Dr. Martin Luther King Jr., Nelson Mandela, and Gandhi, just to name a few. Gandhi was an advocate for racial injustice; he fought the discrimination and racial segregation that Indian immigrants faced in his homeland. The people of India were at the hands and mercy of the white British and Boer authorities. It wasn't until 1894 Gandhi founded the Natal Indian congress to fight discrimination. Gandhi's legal practice consisted of volunteers to help support the British cause so that the Indians could have full rights of citizenship in the British Empire. He encouraged people to be responsible and to fight for justice throughout the land.

Finally, I am one of God's people who is for the people of the world. As a people person, I have nothing but love to give to others.

DORIS GOODMAN

AUTOBIOGRAPHY

My name is Doris Goodman. I am a highly motivated, strong individual who articulates well. I was born in Williamsburg, Brooklyn. My personal background consists of love and an understanding for others. I am very helpful to people, whether they are adults or students. As a concerned individual, I have always held an interest in others.

This is one of the things that makes life so rewarding to me. It's a great feeling to know that I have a love for all people and that I am a naturalist who appreciates others and the things around me. The love and concerns that I possess for others are the most realistic things about myself. I am truly a humanist who supports, promotes, and asserts a plan of action.

As a very positive motivator with goals, guidelines, morals, values, high expectations, and more, I expected no less from my students. As I recall, growing up, I always had a need for more in terms of acquirements. I have always reached for more, even when it appeared to me that I was at the top of my accomplishments. The energy level that I have is the one thing that has made a difference in my personal life because it allows me to evaluate and maintain a strong focus on today's youth.

In my accomplishments, I received recognition in 1988 for creativity in poetry, the Golden Poet award, which was sponsored in Anaheim, California. The poem I received recognition for was published in a book of poems entitled *The Golden Treasury of Great Poems*, John Campbell, editor, and publisher 1989. The title of the poem is "Thank You for Lighting My Fire." I was also selected for nominee at JHS 226, for the Reliance Awards for Excellence in Education, Teacher of the Year in 1991–92. Also, in 1994, I was nominated for teacher of the year through the Walt Disney Company.

In September 1984, I became employed with the NYC Board of Education. When hired as a sixth grade, Special Education Mis II elementary teacher at PS 155 in South Ozone Park, I met a challenge. The first few months were tough, but it was interesting to know that I could turn a negative setting into a positive one. It is important to reach the hearts of the students. I have had the privilege of knowing that I can help students to believe in themselves, maintain respect for themselves and others. This is an accomplishment of mine that exists today.

My influence and stern loving approach have worked for me with people; in fact, the students cooperate because they know I promote excellence in education. This is a special feeling, knowing that I have the ability to make a difference in the lives of an individual especially students.

In June 1996, I applied for a position outside of the classroom. The position in question was the Crisis Intervention Teacher or Coordinator of Special Education. In September 1996 I was granted the position. I had been successfully working almost a year in my new administrative role, which was challenging and quite interesting. This position as CIT reassured my high interest in administration. I was extremely motivated to the point of having a need to better serve the students.

When I arrived on the job, I looked forward to solving problems, delegating with the administration, peers, and parents to meet the needs of the students. This CIT position was rewarding to me in many ways. I knew the positive image that I projected was the one thing that helps me to maintain a balance in my everyday decisions. I can truly see my talents, character, and professional growth prevail from day to day.

In addition to my many experiences, I have learned that environment and the role that the teacher plays will help motivate students. However, the key to an effective school is hard work and team effort. There must be commitment on all parties involved such as the administration staff, teachers, parents, students, and others affiliated with the school. It is important to involve everyone to ensure that students demonstrate success.

For instance, programs, activities, courses in all major subjects, projects, clubs, and more will keep students involved. If students are involved in school or outside the school, there is less chance of them being misled. I would further encourage learning by having the staff teach as early on in the year as possible a need-assessment program, which would involve teaching the students on self-awareness so that they can be made accountable for their actions. The children must know and understand the consequences if they violate the school disciplinary policy. Therefore, an appropriate time to introduce a needs-assessment program would be when students are entering a beginning school year, while obtaining a copy of the school rules and regulations.

Once it is clear that students have read the rules and regulations of the school, I would then begin teaching them academically. In terms of piloting my program, I would include volunteer parents, staff members, and others who certainly believe in the fact that they can make a change in the school system. I would also enhance cooperative learning throughout the entire NYC school system. It is essential that small groups, committees, and communities be designed to help bring about positive change in the school system. This is what helped me be and complete my role as a successful teacher in the Board of Education.

CHAPTER 1

Multicultural Experiences Growing Up and Parents' History throughout the South

When we were created, we were born of many backgrounds. We the people consist of many different backgrounds that cover multicultural tones. We didn't decide who we wanted to be. Thank God because for this, had we decided the race of our choice things could look boring if the people of the world were all the same. It's obvious that if we all wore the same color outfit every day we would get tired of it. If you had a favorite color and that's all you saw, you would get tired of that too. Moreover, if you heard the same music all the time, you would get tired of it as well. The various types of music allow one to engage in a choice, whether it be jazz, rock, gospel, or blues, just to name a few. Therefore, I say to you, as a person we need a variety of choices. All of one kind of a thing or race, this can be a turnoff. It's beautiful to see multicultural backgrounds of people from various countries.

Furthermore, I say to you once again it is possible to initiate change especially if all it only cost you is respect, love, honesty, a peace of mind, or fairness to another human being who doesn't look like you. In my previous examples on how people can become bored if everything was one color, one type of music, or one race of people, how would people truly feel if this was the situation that we were confronted with? If we're not the Creator, why should we pass judgment on others?

I believe people might feel threatened for whatever reason; it is fair to say it's time to change a negative attitude or your opinion about other people who are not like you. I believe people can change; it's all about making a choice. People must be willing to initiate the change. What has happened in this world is sad. People simply don't value the gift of life.

Who said people should be judged by the color of their skin and not by the content of their character?

In addition, the gift of life is only a short time; we come into this world with nothing, and we will leave one day with nothing.

CHAPTER 2

Racism Tried and Failed in My Neighborhood

I can recall when I got my first apartment in Williamsburg, Brooklyn. To this day, I remember the landlord at 92 Morgan Avenue outrightly, boldly, and seriously told me that she didn't want to rent to black people. I was eighteen, desperate and determined to get Delores' apartment, which was the vacant apartment, and the landlady was determined to keep me from getting that apartment.

I grew up on 84 Morgan Avenue. Prior to becoming an adult, I never felt or believed racism existed in my neighborhood because I was surrounded by what I believed was a multicultural environment where people showed love and shared concerns as well as work together. The landlord didn't live in the neighborhood, so I guess being an outsider she was like the rest of the people who had a problem with black folks. However, in reference to the abovementioned, I found a way to get the landlady to change her mind. After all, she didn't know enough about the community to see that it was a tight-knit community where people of all nationalities connected and helped each other thrive. My family and aunts exchanged or, better yet, traded different meals. I remember people helping each other; for instance, my dad would assist a neighbor with car repairs or if someone needed a ride. This was such a good location to grow up in.

This experience I had as a child and a young adult is not compared to where we are in today's world. Moreover, getting back to the landlord who didn't want to rent the apartment to me and my husband, who had just come back home from Vietnam, I told the landlady that my husband and I would keep the building clean. We would set out and pull in the garbage cans, mop and sweep the halls, wipe down the banister, shake the rugs, and keep the lock on the door. It's sad that I had to sell myself; I had to literally clean my way into my first apartment. I not only pushed racism out the door, I also did not accept or allow it to come into the neighborhood that I grew up in.

I never felt racism in my neighborhood until that lady tried to introduce racism. I can't believe I had to fight my way at an early age into my first apartment. I was young and ignorant and didn't know any better. What I do know today is that I pressed and fought my way into a situation that should have never been. I am proud today to say I helped racism back up and make a U-turn.

As my memory serves me, had I not gotten the apartment, the landlady would have won. Who knows, maybe a white tenant could have been prejudiced and I wouldn't be able to recall the love that people shared among each other. It only takes one rotten apple to spoil the bunch.

In sharing my story about applying for my first apartment, it was hard for me to not give up. I am a fighter in a positive way, and it's difficult for me to accept no in anything I do or try to do. I love challenges and will find a way to get my breakthrough. I say to anyone reading this, you must fight in a positive way and never give up. You must think outside the box and come up with positive ideas, ways to prevail and reach your goal.

CHAPTER 3

Racism Thrives if We Allow It

In my opinion, racism will continue to exist if people are not willing for whatever reason to try and understand it's wrong to judge or mistreat people who are not like them. It's been a part of history for years where our ancestors have suffered due to the ignorance and vicious treatment minority people have endured and still to this day are suffering. How long will this hatred go on? Many activists have tried for years to fight for freedom and equality for all races. Many people, such as Martin Luther King Jr., Adam Clayton Power, John Lewis, Rosa Parks, and Harriet Tubman, just to name a few. These people have worked tirelessly for years to help bring about change.

These pioneers have gone on to rest, and so not much has changed in the matter of racism. Therefore, the fight continues as people struggle in this country to be treated with respect, fairly and equally. This is a fight that can be eliminated if people stand up and initiate change. What would happen if the shoe was on the other foot? It's a shame people have died fighting for freedom, something that should come automatically. It's obvious that certain groups of people have to prove themselves worthy when it comes to getting a job or moving into a certain neighborhood or position.

Many times, people form their opinion, or they pass judgment on others who are not like them. Why? When does it stop? It seems unfair that life is so unfair to certain groups of people. People need to respect God's creation; I believe this was God's choice. Who gives people the right to discriminate?

CHAPTER 4

The Kickback on Racism Is Worth Today's Challenge

My parents were born in Alabama in 1928. My father would tell me stories about what it was like growing up in the South. I learned how he had to adapt to segregation, which involved hate and mistreatment of black people, who is said to be considered one particular minority group.

My father talked about separate bathrooms, water fountains, churches, neighborhoods, and much more, just to name a few. My mother's stories were similar to my father's. If you lived in the South during my parents' era from 1938 to late 1940s, you were not able to be integrated at one point in time, and as a growing young boy, my father told me he had expressed to his father that the man he was doing business with drove his pickup truck very close to him in an attempt to run him over. This was a child's perception, so his father dismissed the child's story; perhaps business was more important to his father at that time; this was a Caucasian man.

At the time, a lot of hatred was going on, and my father's dad could only be glad for the business the man was giving him. Many times, children are told to be quiet or convinced to believe the opposite of what he or she experienced even if they know the truth. My father said he had never forgotten that experience as a child. There was so much going on in the South; people suffered at the hands of some of the Caucasians. Many people were beaten and killed, all because of racism and hatred. Black people were attacked by dogs and beaten by the police department.

As time went on, my parents grew up and eventually moved north. My father was the first to move to New York City. He did not know my mother because they lived in different locations of Alabama. My father was from Sardis, Alabama, and my mother was from Autaugaville, Alabama, so they did not know each other in the South. My mother attended Tuskegee Institute National Historic Site located in Alabama.

As time went on, my mother decided to take a trip to New York City. It is my belief that my grandmother was surprised that once she arrived in New York for what was supposed to be a short vacation. I believe New York City was exciting, interesting, and appealing enough to make a person want to explore the city, especially coming from a small city like Autaugaville in Alabama.

My mother's family was able to send her to college. After my mother's first year in college, she took a trip to New York City, where she later met my father; at that point, college for my mother became history. My mother stayed in New York with her older brothers. The area in which she and her brothers lived was in Williamsburg, Brooklyn, on Morgan Avenue. This is where the family resided.

In addition, Morgan Avenue became a place where family members eventually relocated. It seemed like one family found out about this place and they decided to move into the area as well. Knowing what I know today about racism I, don't blame them for coming together as a family of love. Morgan Avenue, Brooklyn, had nothing but love, families helping each other, and making every effort to live in harmony. After all that black people went through, I guess living in an area where people pulled together is what made them so unique and special. Morgan Avenue did not just consist of family members, there were several different races of people. I knew that the area was mixed with Caucasians, Hispanics, Germans, Italians, Mexicans, and Jews.

As time went on, my mother met my father. They got married eventually, later leading to them having five children. The first child, my brother, was born in 1949; I was born 1950, my second brother was born 1953, my sister 1955, and my last sister 1957. Most of my aunts and uncles had children who also lived on Morgan Avenue. There was never a time where we were lonely, bored, or without someone to play with. We were and still are a blessed family. As an adult today, I can attest to the strengths and the love we had growing up; the love was sweet, fulfilling, and precious. As we experienced this, we were also surrounded by caring families.

The families who did not live on Morgan Avenue would come over every now and then. There were so many aunts, uncles, and cousins, it always felt like a big block party. My father came from a family of thirteen-plus that my father's mother raised. My mother had six brothers, and she was the only girl.

A few of my first cousins who lived on Morgan Avenue

CHAPTER 5

Racism Existed Minimally in My Neighborhood

In addition to the family, there were multiple groups of people living on Morgan Avenue who were not related. As I mentioned earlier in my writing, we got along with the Germans, Italians, Jews, Hispanics, Mexicans, and Caucasian families. In fact, one of the Caucasian families gave my brother his nickname, which is Lover, and we still call him Lover to this day. My family exchanged different foods with many of the people living on Morgan Avenue. This blended culture that I once knew; I have not experienced it like when I was growing up. The cultures that I believed in showed respect, love, and honesty.

It's apparent to me that I experienced a multicultural upbringing that to this day stayed with me as an adult. There are people in this world who can talk about having a hard life while growing up. My memories of the past in a particular neighborhood were good ones. I recall neighbors working together. The people showed love, respect, and peace toward one another. I was fortunate and blessed to have experienced a background of my families and friends living together in harmony.

As a child, I observed people getting along, working together, and helping each other. I was that child who noticed everything, I could see so many families pulling their resources together, showing and caring about one another. This was love to me, and this stayed with me. I'm often reminded of where I came from and how different it is today. Blended cultures, that's what I once knew.

This lifestyle that I experienced while growing up, I have yet to see again. There are many races of people that show love today toward one another but nothing like how it was growing up. The people were close knitted; they had respect and love, and they were honest.

As a child growing up, I watched families work with other people who were not like them; it seems to me color did not matter to the people; there was love and respect for one another. In regard to the view of the past multicultural experiences, there is no comparison to how life was while growing up on Morgan Avenue, Brooklyn. The life I once knew brings tears to my eyes; with what I know today about racism, it's more than a shame when people react toward one another because they are not like them. It's sad, and it hurts to know that people can be so indifferent to another race of people.

Moreover, I knew growing up on Morgan Avenue racism existed minimally as opposed to the outskirts of that neighborhood. I knew when I was at school racism was in the school. I remember myself and a few of my cousins were chased to where we lived, and that was to Morgan

Avenue, Brooklyn. I was in middle school, eighth grade at Enrico Fermi, when a rumor was spread, and I heard it. The rumor was "The niggers are in the gym, let's get them." We were chased all the way home. Also, there were times when cousins would leave the block and experience racism in the park. There would be other people fighting for the handball court; it did not matter if you were there first, it boiled down to who was going to play handball.

My point is that racism existed while growing up but outside of my neighborhood. Morgan Avenue was a special place back in the early 1960s; many people who lived on the between streets of Morgan Avenue such as Grattan Street, Harrison Place, Johnson Avenue, Knickerbocker Avenue, and Ingram Avenue came around to Morgan Avenue. In fact, I met my first husband on Morgan Avenue; he lived on one of the side streets, Grattan Street, which I mentioned.

This Williamsburg Morgan Avenue was like a community block party filled with a love connection. People just learned about the area, and they showed up. There was enough business in the area such as delis, restaurants, candy shops, banks, bars, subways, and coffee shops to draw people in. As people came and went, it was almost like an open marketplace where you took care of your business and then went on about your business.

It was God's choice when he created man; who gave or gives people the right to judge others based on the color of their skin? The human being was created by God. He decided on the multicultural backgrounds of the people. God's decision was what you see, what you know, and what it is.

Therefore, as a people of the world, we should be equal regardless of our color; we should not have to fight to get what we deserve as a people. God gave the people of the world a gift; we have the gift of life through God's creation. It is important for people to realize this gift of life can be in many backgrounds, which once again consists of blended cultures.

CHAPTER 6

Many Activists Fought in the Past for Equality

In addition to the abovementioned persons, concerned with racism in the past, Arthur Ashe was one who always felt the need to try and help people of color, freedom, and equal rights. He felt a need like many others to try and help bring about change in reference to people's rights.

Arthur Ashe believed black people should be free to go about making positive decisions. As he was driving across the George Washington Bridge, he heard on the radio Dr. Martin Luther King Jr was killed in Memphis, Tennessee, located at the Lorraine Motel in April 1968. This was a tragedy that led to a ball of confusion for many people, black and white. People were distraught behind Martin Luther King Jr.'s death. Many riots took place in various states; people were angry, sad, revengeful, and frustrated with the way the sign of the times displayed hatred among various groups of people.

Moreover, as time went on, Arthur Ashe felt compelled to do something to help enlighten humanity by using his voice. He spoke to groups of people, held meetings as well as spoke to children. Ashe was a strong believer of people's rights and freedom. He held meetings to enlighten people of their rights and help empower them and find their voice. He felt it was imperative that people stand up for their rights and voice their opinion and not be passive in life.

Arthur Ashe did not want to be remembered just as a tennis player. He strived throughout life, traveled to various places including South Africa, where he met Nelson Mandela, who was against the policies of apartheid in the twentieth century during which Nelson Mandela was incarcerated for twenty-seven years and spent time between Robben Island and Pollsmoor prison and Victor Vester prison.

Nelson and Arthur Ashe did not meet in person until after the apartheid regime had fallen; it was then that the two engaged in a friendship that resulted in transcended ideas and different political and physical barriers. Both Ashe and Nelson worked toward the eradication system. Mandela focused through his protest and activism while he was jailed. Arthur Ashe implemented his efforts to expel South Africa from the International Lawn Tennis Foundation and athletes against the apartheid. As time passed there was a South African Open. Nelson Mandela and Arthur Ashe camaraderie continued until Ashe's death.

Arthur Ashe associated humanity with Andrew Young and many others. He was not just a former tennis player. He used his voice, his wisdom, and his ability to empower people as well as dealing with the youth. Arthur Ashe did not allow his health to stop him from fighting for what he called freedom and equal rights in spite of his heart attack in 1979. He continued to work prior to his death on February 6, 1993, wherein he died of AIDS due to a blood transfusion. He was a well-known social activist who gained the respect of thousands of people. He was the only African American man to win Wimbledon; his opponent was Jimmy Connors. Ashe also played at the US and Australian Open. His health problems developed; he retired from tennis, but he was inducted into the International Tennis Hall of Fame in 1985.

Activist Abernathy, 3/11/1926-4/7/1990

Ralph David Abernathy was active in the National Association for the Achievement of Colored People and cheered the state school and Baptists Training Union Congress Committee on *Brown vs. Board of Education*. Abernathy was also affiliated with the Martin Luther King Jr. Research and Education Institute. Abernathy was born on March 11, 1926, and died on April 7, 1990. He was against segregation; he urged minorities to fight against segregation. In 1957, his church and him were bombed. Last but not least, the late Bill Russell, known for two NBA championships, also voiced his beliefs about racism. He said everyone should be equal, and he wasn't content in the struggle for civil rights.

The director of the anti-racist research and policies center at American University, according to Ibram X, Kendi explains the opposite of "racist" isn't "not racist"; he says it is "anti-racist." According to the article by Anna North,

June 3, 2020, 1:50 p.m., it's not enough to be racist; also Kendi notes it's not enough to be not racist.

Kendi explains the opposite of racist and it isn't "not racist"; he writes, "It's antiracist" It has been said that the focus on anti-racism has been the attention recently as Americans throughout the country rise up against the police violence. Also, civil rights work by black Americans according to Malini Ranganathan, a faculty team lead at the anti-racist research and policy center. It was also said by Kendi and others according to the term antiracist he describes it as more than a fight against racism or said to be nonracist. Antiracism means eradicating policies that are racist and have racist outcomes. Ranganathan said policies should work toward a more egalitarian emancipatory society.

Another comment was made by a white woman who said she can't experience what it feels like to experience racism but to fight against it as a person of color; she went on to say people of color should not be responsible to correct or fix racism or to explain to whites not to be racist. Dina Simmons is a scholar, practitioner of social-emotional learning and equity, and also the author of the upcoming book "White Rules for Black People."

She explains, "Don't ask the wounded to do the work." She talked to experts on the topic to help others, including herself; she explains how important it is to know what antiracism means and how it should be a common practice. Simmons goes on to say white folks always want to know how they can do better. Simmons said, "I say start by doing something."

CHAPTER 7

Diversified Community and Families Sharing Food and Recipes

Growing up in a diversified community certainly helped enhance my lifestyle; I remember meeting people of all nationalities. It's good to know I was fortunate to experience different races during my childhood. My diversified experience gives me hope, strength, and the ability to reach out and help people in many ways. The diversity allowed me to assist people of different ethnic and cultural backgrounds. My diverse experience not only played a role in my child experience but also helped pave the road right into my adult life.

I believe being exposed to diversity at an early age helped make every bit of my life successful today, on the job and in the community. Also, it's important to realize the connections people make in an early life can benefit them in more ways than one. There's an old saying, "You act like what you are around." In other words, the company you keep can influence your lifestyle. It's always important to assess yourself, know yourself and believe that success is waiting on you if people trust and believe in themselves.

It is also the responsibility for people to plan their lifestyle so they might have an opportunity to meet people with different backgrounds with the hope of making a difference in the world. There are opportunities through social gatherings, jobs, church functions, neighborhoods, and traveling to various places where people are of different ethnicities as opposed to being complacent. I believe that experiencing other cultures and finding similarities within your own will bring understanding that can bring people closer. There is opportunity in life if we people just take advantage of what's available to them in their environment. Also, people can reach out to people to learn about various resources that they can consider in order to bring about change in themselves as well as the world.

Growing up in such a diverse neighborhood, I soon realized many families had customs like our own, especially when it came to celebration. One custom in particular that stood out to me was the importance of food and how certain dishes had significant meaning behind it. I recall people of color pooling together to make a meal out of leftovers, soup bones, vegetables, and plenty of scraps. There was a time when family and neighbors shared food recipes to give each other an opportunity to experience what each other's food taste like.

I have a fond memory of this lovely Italian woman named Betty who lived on Morgan Avenue. One particular time, Betty sent my cousin Norma, who was twelve at the time, to the butcher for groceries; the butcher also prepared a bag for my cousin's mom, and as Norma left the butcher, she accidentally mixed up the bags, and Betty received the wrong bag. When Betty opened her bag up, she would then find scraps of meat and bones. Betty was furious, so she gathered Norma, and they stormed back to the butcher, and she insisted that he would never do that again; the butcher was known for passing off scraps of meat to families of color.

A few times during the holidays, Betty would share her Italian dishes with my aunt Tee, and Tee would share her pan of corn bread. There were Spanish families who gave my mom and aunt rice and beans with chicken. In return, my mom and sometimes my aunt shared a Southern dish called greens. Also, during the holidays, especially New Year's, black families would prepare a hog head of pork, along with other cultural dishes. My mom and aunts would send dishes to another member or neighbor to taste and enjoy. The hog head was a traditional dish that was mostly prepared on the first day of the new year. This hog head was also prepared with black-eyed peas, collard greens, corn bread, yams, and mac and cheese. Along with potato salad as part of the meal for the first day of new year. However, the main traditional dish was hog head, greens, black-eyed peas, and corn bread.

The history behind this New Year's dish was said to be a common practice. The greens and black-eye peas were for good luck and prosperity for the upcoming year. The meal was a practice that goes all the way back to the Civil War. So then people were left with fewer crops in the field, greens and black-eyed peas were seen as a nutrient source that was said to be rich and was used during the winter months mostly.

The hog head was popular in the South; pigs were considered a sign of good eating and prosperity when times were hard. Therefore, pork represented progress, and it fed families for days, weeks, and longer. This food—hog head, black-eyed peas, and greens—is what black families carried wherever they resided. Then there was the Spanish-style pork shoulder known as pernil, which was shared to other cultures. As a young adult, I would prepare the pork shoulder in place of the hog head.

In addition to all the foods mentioned above, I had an opportunity to eat at some of my friends' homes. I grew up eating a variety of multicultural foods at my neighbor's house; my cousins and I would go from house to house, tasting and eating various dishes as well as eating our parent's food. I was influenced so much by these cultures that I even began trying to replicate these dishes.

CHAPTER 8

The Life I Once Knew Brings Tears to My Eyes with What I Know Now

There was a time when life seemed to be easier and safer as I recall growing up. There was minimum crime on the streets; people seemed to be more relaxed and open-minded. I remember when I bought my first house at the age of twenty-one in Laurelton Queens on Francis Lewis Boulevard. I recall never locking my doors; my screen door in the seventies was never locked. I believe the reason I felt comfortable enough to leave my doors open was due to my upbringing in Williamsburg. On Morgan Avenue, once again where I grew up, there were family, neighbors, and friends whom I was surrounded by and a community that protected me. This must have carried over into my adult life. It was a beautiful feeling, catching this summer breeze and watching the stars in the early evening. I was a latchkey child; I was at home after school with my brothers, Duke and Lover, along with my two sisters, Christine and Ruth.

There were five of us, two brothers and two sisters, including myself. Adolf Junior was the oldest of the five siblings. He was born on April 24, 1949; he was known as Duke; he got that nickname because he liked to box—yes everywhere he went or who he came in contact with. He loved to box, so the nickname Duke stuck on him. Duke was very different in a unique way; he dressed a certain way. His style of clothes consisted of yellow dress slacks, all-American V-neck sweaters, penny loafers, white dress shirts, Italian shoes, suspenders, along with cuffs in his pants.

Duke's style of clothes was different from the neighborhood. The neighborhood boys did not dress the same way; the fashion for other males was with sneakers, jeans, and T-shirts. Duke's music was different; he enjoyed jazz; he listened to the Symphony Sid show. Sid was known for his charisma; there were other jazz DJs, but no one could outwit Sid. Sid had a slogan, "I dig you the most." Symphony Sid's last few years on radio in NYC on the FM station I believe to be WRVR. Duke also had a way with people; besides wanting to box all the time, in addition to this, he was a great socialist. He had a beautiful smile that took him places.

Duke got around; he worked in the neighborhood, and he managed to get around the outskirts of other areas. Me, being his sister, gave me power. I always felt protected and special because people would always say, "That's Duke sister." Duke loved to dance; he had a smooth way of dancing on the dance floor; he could spin you around and dip you, never letting you go. The music and the hustle was the biggest thing aside from jazz.

The rest of the four siblings fell under the normal average child with the exception of myself. I benefited by being the oldest girl and being close to Duke. I got a lot of attention, thanks to Duke. We danced and we joked. I was able to meet some of Duke's friends. I worked part-time when school was out. I was able to obtain some of my clothes and shoes for school. Although I was shy with socializing, whenever a party was happening, I managed to dance with Duke; he was the party—he brought the crowd to the party.

Moreover, no matter what fun we had growing up, I never neglected my studies; in fact, I was a bookworm, as they say. I helped others with their studies; this seemed to always be a part of me. I love life and nice things in life. I was particular when it came to spending money. I knew my family was not rich. I knew we didn't always have the things that other families had. The love in the family was a great motivation to me. I was not surrounded with the best material things, but family love helped me realize I can always obtain whatever we didn't have growing up, providing that I got a good education and job.

I learned early in life there is always the possibility of obtaining one's desires in life; in other words, it takes planning, patience, and having a goal that can be measured. It's important to observe how well the goal is being progressed. The goal must be measured to ensure that one will be able to be successful.

My younger brother and sister were, in my opinion, ordinary children as we were all growing up; however, the one thing that I knew, we were a loving family, and no one was better than the other. I felt a need to obtain more in life, and I had a need to broaden my skills in a positive manner. As I planned early in life, my education, which included my goals, I was able to have a comfortable lifestyle. Although obstacles occurred in my life, which allowed me to learn from them, it was my determination and drive in me that helped me maintain the lifestyle I live today.

As you continue to read about how to ensure a lifestyle that provides you with success, it's important to realize early in life to save and plan your goals. It's important to put money away for the future, discipline yourself, avoid being wasteful with your money even if you have to pay yourself every time you pay bills. It's important that people develop good habits early in life so tomorrow is well established with their finances, and you can be prepared if an emergency occurs.

There was no adult supervision; we were dismissed from school and arrived home. We turned the doorknob and waited for our parents to come home. This was our daily routine; there were plenty of families and friends in the community who watched out for us. It felt strange not having a key because I saw other kids with the key around their necks; as a kid, we never had a key to open the house door and no parents to greet us until a couple of hours after we had gotten home.

Therefore, living a lifestyle of this magnitude was one of a kind. In today's world, one not only better have a key but also an alarm system as well as lighting around your house. In today's world, there seems to be more crime and death. It is apparent to me that people are threatened, attacked, and murdered for no reason. Crime is increasing at such an accelerated pace that it is all the media outlets report about; every day the news depicts some sort of a crime. There was crime in the past but not like today; the media seems to consistently inform the public about a senseless crime. There is more crime in the subway, parks, and banks.

Also, there are random attacks today by some people who are suffering from mental illness, or this is them using it as a cop-out. People appear to be angrier today than yesterday; the lack of safety has accelerated, and people seem to be short fused as opposed to defusing a situation before it gets out of control. We had crime in the past, but once again not to the extent of what we have today. It is my belief that a contributing factor to increase in crime is due to a lot of people being jobless and living on the street; I believe that this is a big part of the problem. People are getting shot in their homes by stray bullets penetrating their walls or hit as a bystander on the street. I'm sure without a doubt about crime there's no comparison today as that of the past.

The public is fighting for the gun laws to be approved so that people can obtain a gun legally. It appears that everyone wants to own a gun today in order to protect themselves. This was not the issue in the past; I know some people had guns, but not like it is today. Also, there have been multiple shootings in various schools such as Uvalde, Texas, a mass shooting that left eighteen students and one teacher dead;

Columbine High School, Littleton, Colorado, thirteen victims killed by two gunmen who went on a shooting spree on April 20, 1999, and twelve students and a teacher plus twenty others wounded.

In 2005, seven victims at Red Lake Senior High school in Minnesota. On March 21, 2005, a sixteen-year-old gunman did the crime and later died by suicide. Also, West Nickel Mine School in Nickel Mines, Pennsylvania, where a shooting took place; the gunman shot five girls and then turned the gun on himself. On April 16, 2007, Virginia Tech, killing thirty-two victims. Then there was a senseless shooting at Sandy Hook Elementary in Newtown, Connecticut. Twenty-six victims killed in 2012 in Oikos University; in 2012 another shooting took place, killing seven victims, along with one staff member. There are so many others, it'll take days to get through all of them.

Therefore, with factual evidence revealing lives lost due to illegal guns or lack of gun safety regulations, this confirms how crime rates have increased today as opposed to the past. This is a horrendous condition. This is definitely a sign of the times, and it proves how drastically things are in terms of crime. It is a fact that crime is up and innocent people are being killed.

In comparison to what I knew growing up, I never heard of crime as much as I hear about it today. I know back during my upbringing people had guns; I also know crime took place, but I didn't know crime back then like I know it today. In today's world, crime is out of control: people dodging bullets, and people losing loved ones due to someone else's negligence. It has been said it's too easy to purchase a gun nowadays; it wasn't that easy years ago to get guns. Today people purchase guns like buying candy. It's also a fact that teenagers have been able to purchase guns; these babies are killing others and themselves. Whatever happened to a fist fight? We did this years ago if it was necessary when having a dispute; the fight left you sore, but you were alive.

Brooklyn Bridge

CHAPTER 9

One Memory of the Past Spoiled a Barrel of Many Memories

As time passed on, families in the community continued to work together and be helpful to one another. It was such a joy watching how neighbors, family, and friends pulled together. There was much love and respect that was shared by everyone; this was a community with a love connection filled with hope and prosperity for the future. People who lived in the neighborhood had plans; there seemed to be a drive in the people to do better for themselves and their children. The people worked hard to make a difference. The families made sure myself and others like me were prepared for the future; the adults encouraged myself and their children to strive for the better things in life.

Although the people in the neighborhood tried to keep a safe environment, there was always something that could happen or come up beyond one's control. What I am about to disclose to you no one saw it coming; there was not even a sign of trouble approaching no one could imagine what I'm about to tell you. This was an unbelievable crime that happened on August 1, 1973.

The weather was hot, sunny, and it was a beautiful day. The whole neighborhood was outside, taking in those beautiful blue skies along with the heat from the sun, and everyone was enjoying themselves. I had moved away from Morgan Avenue because my husband and I purchased our first house.

I then got a call telling me to come quick; my brother had just been shot and killed on Morgan Avenue in Brooklyn. This was a blow not only to the community but also to our family. This was horrible, cold, mean, and unnecessary. This shooting caused an uproar in the community. Family and friends were angry; there were police and detectives throughout the entire neighborhood. It was the darkest and saddest day of all days. Adolph Smiley Jr. a.k.a. Duke was well-liked by family and friends. He had a tremendous impact on the community. He was an extraordinary person who reached out to people.

Duke worked for a man named Izzy. Duke was smart and left such an impression on his boss, Izzy, that he wanted to send him to college; unfortunately, he never made it. I can say that Duke had a great taste for clothing; he had an impeccable character with good ideas for fashion. There was no one in our community that could touch his style of dressing; Duke had a preppy appearance of dressing. He wore at times an all-American sweater, yellow pants, and Italian shoes, just to name a few personal pieces of clothing. He had a style of his own; no one could outdress him or measure up to the drive he had in him. He loved the show called *The Symphony Sid Show* that played jazz during the early seventies.

I learned the facts that led up to my brother's death. It was said that my brother Duke had an argument with two young men when they came into the community on Morgan Avenue. The men lived outside of Morgan Avenue; however, my brother knew them. Whatever they were arguing about is unclear to me; I did hear that Duke had the upper hand with the dispute. The men became angrier, and they used the term, "Your mother," in order to retaliate based on what Duke was saying to them. Once Duke heard that term, the fight broke out; it then was on and popping, as one might say.

Duke whipped the two men, not realizing they both had revolvers. The men shot and killed my brother Duke in broad daylight with the presence of family watching. Shots fired, screams rang out, with people running and ducking for shelter while screaming for help. The sad part is a life was taken over an argument.

Duke was twenty-two years old, and he lost his life over an argument that could have been settled in a different way. The irony of the argument was death took precedence over one's life. What a tragic loss! Much like today, certain terms are used to provoke one another, and back in the seventies, saying, "Your mother," was an ultimate sign of disrespect.

CHAPTER 10

Excerpts from Morgan Avenue Residents

Leroy Smiley

Hey, this is Leroy Smiley, and I just wanted to let you know my opinion on coming up in the 1960s as far as the type of neighborhood it was compared to the neighborhoods of today. I grew up in a neighborhood where we had white people, Spanish people, black people, and different kinds of ethnic groups. Morgan Avenue was diverse; we had Jews, Germans, Italians, Hispanic, Latino, and Afro American. It was just a cool neighborhood; you had some people that were racist, and you had people that weren't; there were a couple of families that later moved into the neighborhood that made it clear that you weren't welcome.

I feel like I was blessed because you grow up in a neighborhood like that you learned to recognize who racist people are. You learned who liked you or loved you for who you were and that's the way it was. I had a lot of friends and a lot of white friends that came from diverse backgrounds.

You just learned when you go to certain people's houses and how they treat you, and you go to other people houses, and you feel like they really don't want you there; in one instance, I was told to get out.

There were also neighborhoods that we couldn't go in such as Bensonhurst or Ridgewood; the white people would chase us if we went out there. There were neighborhoods where white people couldn't go in black neighborhoods, and it was just crazy, but on Morgan Avenue, that little enclave on Morgan Avenue was like, "Hey, this is R&R, rest and relaxation."

We don't care who you are or what your color is; if you live on Morgan Avenue or are within the vicinity, it's going to be cool. People looked out for you, and that's the way it was. I'm going to have a little bit more to tell you in the future, but for now, I'm signing off.

Samuel Little

What is racism, or racist? Here's what seventy-five years of experience has taught me about the actions between two or more people on the subject of race. *Racist* is a term I started using later in life and have applied to actions of people I thought to be racist. As a young male growing up in Green Point New York, north of Flushing Avenue in a Spanish-Speaking neighborhood and south of Flushing Avenue down knickerbocker Avenue the heart of an Italian Community.

My junior high school PS 162 in Ridgewood, New York, was a melting pot of German, Italian, Spanish, Black, and Polish students. Many whom I call friends and some my protectors, because the population of blacks was in the minority and were not a threat to any of the other groups. At the time, I had not developed an opinion on race. Even though I was a witness to the constant conflict between the Spanish and Italian student body. They just did not like each other, and at the time, I did not think of it as a race problem. That's a label I would place on it today, the current time.

At Forty-Nine Grattan Street, the building I lived in, there were six apartments, all occupied by black families and entirely surrounded by buildings occupied by Spanish-speaking families. I can't recall anyone in my building saying a harsh word about another family. My neighborhood was lively and a fun place to grow up in.

Knickerbocker Avenue was the local shopping center. Retailers, one supermarket, a butcher shop, and the Starr integrated movie house serviced our inter-racial communities. Shopkeepers knew my mother on a first-name basis; whenever she walked past a shop, the owner made it a point to step outside to speak. Many of their children were classmates. Two in particular I want to mention here. Franky's parents owned a shoe store; they did not speak, nor could they hear but were two of the nicest people I ever met. Very friendly toward me and my family. Often, Franky and I would walk together home from school. The route up knickerbocker Avenue went past his family's shoe store, and I would spend time with them before going home.

My other friend Larry was a different story. I had never met nor spoken to any member of his family. According to Larry, his Italian parents, the same race as Franky would not tolerate him having a black friend. I accepted Larry's statement as fact and never questioned it; he was my friend and frequently spent time at my parents' home. In those days, this was the world we lived in. The topic of racism was not as much an open conversation as it is today. We overlooked some of the bad behavior of others and viewed it as normal.

Larry was not my only encounter with accepting action that might be labeled racist today. During my days in the military a Puerto Rican platoon classmate and I were rewarded weekend passes after passing a physical training test. Both of us being from New York decided to travel by train home from South Carolina. Traveling in our dressed uniforms, we entered the front door of the station and seated ourselves; the attendant approached and informed us that we were not allowed to wait in that area. That we had to wait on the platform in the back of the station. We accepted that and did not question the why because we understood this was the world we lived in at the time.

Lester C. Smith

It was September 1965 I was fifteen years old, and the school year had just begun in Brooklyn. I was enrolled in the eighth grade at Junior High School 145, in the Bushwick section of Brooklyn. My brother Vernard (Footie), although we both lived in the very same house, we went to different schools. Footie was enrolled in the seventh grade at Junior High School 111, also in the Bushwick section of Brooklyn.

In my teens I was constantly in all types of trouble in and outside of school. I was classified as a "juvenile delinquent." My behavior outside of school caused me to get arrested and locked up. I spent two weeks in the Bronx Youth House (a detention center for juvenile delinquents). When I returned to school, the principal transferred me out of JHS 145, into JHS 111.

Footie and I, up until I was fifteen, had totally different friends. My friends were just like I was habitually committing criminal acts; on the other hand, Footie and his friends were just the opposite. Their interest centered around hanging out, going to parties, and chasing girls. Footie was extremely handsome and was an extraordinary dancer. After getting transferred to JHS 111, I made my mind up to stay out of trouble, so I started hanging out with Footie. There was a pizza shop across the street from JHS 111 that has a jukebox, where the boys and girls would have pizza after school and dance; in addition, Footie along with his friends and a lot of girls, on Friday after school went to a Wesleyan Church on Bushwick Avenue that had a Bible study, after which the minister played music and the boys and girls danced; obviously we were not there to study the Bible.

I first saw Yvonne Marie (Yvonne) as she was dancing after school with her then boyfriend, and Yvonne could really dance. I asked Footie, "Who is that girl?" and he said, "Oh, that's Yvonne and she lives down in the Bottom."

Actually, she lived on Johnson Avenue; however, most of her family members lived on Morgan Avenue, which Footie and his friends designated as the Bottom because when you crossed Flushing Avenue, which ran parallel to Johnson Avenue, that stretch of blocks of Morgan Avenue between Flushing Avenue and Johnson Avenue Footie and his friends called that the Bottom.

I told Footie that I thought Yvonne was fine. He said to me not only is she fine but her cousins Doris (Lee-Sister), Dorothy (Sister), and Carol were also fine. Each time after that when I went to school, I looked forward to getting a chance to dance with Yvonne. I never spoke to her letting her know how I felt about her.

One Sunday afternoon in October, I went to a school yard on Arion Place near Bushwick Avenue. I met up with Footie; when I got there, Footie told me that Yvonne's boyfriend had just broken up with her. I told Footie, "Let's go down to the Bottom." I don't know how he knew that Yvonne was at her aunt Ann's house having her hair done. When we got there, I called Yvonne's name as loud as I could, and she came outside where I was. As she walked over to me, I pulled her close to me and said, "From now on, you go with me." She responded, "Okay."

I kissed her. She then turned around and went back into her aunt's house. That following Monday at school, we hooked up, and every day, we were together until we married on Friday, August 18, 1967. As of this writing, we have celebrated fifty-five years of marriage; we have three awesome children and six precious grandchildren.

In addition to the excerpts, in spite of everything that was happening in the neighborhood such as people working together sharing and caring about one another getting along and demonstrating a peaceful environment on Morgan Ave in the Williamsburg section of Brooklyn, which they nicknamed the area down in the bottom where Lester Smith, met my cousin Yvonne Marie which was on Morgan Avenue, but nicknamed down in the Bottom, which was where Yvonne spent lots of time due to family living on Morgan Avenue in Williamsburg, Brooklyn.

It was not only a family affair; it was friends as well as family coming together. Whether they came from downtown, uptown, or any of the five boroughs, they ended up on Morgan Avenue, which was definitely a safe haven.

CHAPTER 11

Referencing Juneteenth: Annette Gordon-Reed

Referencing the book *On Juneteenth* by Annette Gordan Reed. Reed depicts that equality is still a struggle for black people today as well as in connection with the past history. She talks about how racial inequality was wrong in reality and in film, making as well as in the community. Annette Gordan Reed reveals the racial intolerance in filmmaking; she describes the lack of tolerance and the intolerance in the community.

In addition, Annette G. Reed reveals there is evidence of how white people in Texas during the 1800s forced the Indians off the land and then in turn used the black people who were slaves to tend to the land by planting and harvesting crops. The whites were said to have romanticized the slave women.

It was said the civilization of five tribes—Cherokee, Chickasaw, Choctaw Creek, and Seminole—enslaved blacks as well. They held a racist attitude like the whites. In fact, Cynthia Parker was kidnapped in 1836 as a young girl. She was adopted into the Comanche tribe, and eventually, she was named a Comanche chief for years and had three children. Parker lived with the Comanche until the Texas Rangers recaptured her and forced her to live again with Anglo-Americans. It was then that the white settlers had begun to intrude on their territory, causing many raids which the Comanche carried out against white settlers and the Native American tribes.

As Annette Gordan Reed continues to write many memoirs, she gives a historical account; she states that blacks were not viewed as true Americans. It was said that blacks were rejected and cannot be true Americans. It appears that black people allowed themselves to go along with what was said or told to them in the past. It appears that whites created what was a negative connotation against blacks. Whites used their numbers to create a law as well as a policy. Also, a quote from W. E. B. Du Bois states that the souls of black people identified as the dilemma black people faced in the United States. It was said that blackness and Americans were cast as opposites to one another. This was generated by history and the desires of others. In 1903, Du Bois felt he had a right to focus on black double consciousness, making them believe they were accepted.

Moreover, the Supreme Court case involving *Plassey vs. Ferguson* concerning race, segregating separate but equal tracks failed between the black race; in other words, considering first-class citizenship and second-class citizenship still was not fair. Many blacks helped build this country even though many of their fellow countryman failed to credit their ability. It seems that Texas planned to stand alone during the period 1730–1760s. They refused to accept the fact that they were exceptional as they stood alone in their beliefs and thinking.

In concluding my narrative on racism, I'd like to emphasize the importance of being able to feel free in life. Human beings come in multiple colors, consisting of various ethnic backgrounds. I'd like to emphasize the importance of being able to feel free in life—in other words, being able to live and make decisions as a result of one's independence and freedom of speech. As opposed to having one's rights taken away because they were enslaved, sold, or had no rights due to slavery, this act of injustice forfeits the right for people to feel free. Therefore, when God created man, this alone should have granted people equal rights. The birth of life is a gift if people recognize life as a gift; maybe they would have a whole new perspective on life. In other words, people might learn to respect others who are not like them, and people of different nationalities might be willing to learn from each other as opposed to groups believing they are superior to other people who are not like them.

Many years ago, as well as today, black people have always had to fight for their rights to be free and equal to having the same rights as white people. I, like other activists, do not believe in segregation. In the beginning of time, integration should have been accepted for all races. People should not have had to fight to be accepted in life. If people qualify for jobs, titles, or any other administrative positions, they should not be judged by the color of their skin.

It's hard to believe we are not there yet; we still have mountains to climb, rivers to cross, and barriers to break.

It's hard to believe in today's world people show hatred, prejudice, and meanness to some people. This doesn't apply to everyone, but every now and again, you hear stories about people being disrespected, ignored, or brushed off because of who they are. It's important for people to be successful in life, and a person's well-being contributes to success. When people know that they are part of the environment that they live in and have equal rights that ofter an opportunity to all mankind, they can be hopeful in life as opposed to feeling rejected.

It's imminent that all people should have the same rights which are inherited through birth. This should be a form of protection to mankind, not just to certain groups of individuals who believe they have the right to overlook certain people who are not like them or who cannot protect themselves. The struggle toward civil rights goes back during slavery times; however, the civil rights movement became a strong action by many black leaders during the 1950s to end segregation and discrimination. I'd like to say the world has been fighting to end segregation it was finally seen by the NAACP leaders and African American leaders to fight for desegregation.

Martin Luther King Jr., a leader of nonviolence, along with Mohammed Gandhi and other followers, joined in the struggle for people of India to gain independence from the British. There were several policies throughout the nation that rallied support nationwide fighting for civil rights. Dr. King was elected president in 1957 of the Southern Christian Leadership Conference in Atlanta, Georgia, by church leaders from all over the South. Congress got involved and past a Civil Rights Act to enforce voting rights. Also, African American college students in 1960 fought segregation in Greensboro, North Carolina. As people protested, they were beaten and arrested but maintained nonviolence. This committee included members of all races in 1961, another organization when the Congress of racial equality attempted to enforce integration on interstate buses. There were black and white people protesting for racial equality, which was eventually achieved.

CHAPTER 12

Learning the History of Jane Bolin

As I continue to write, it's important to further tell my story. As time goes on, history still remains the same. People of color have been denied, rejected, or mistreated in more ways than one over a period of time. In some instances, there have been opportunity, a breakthrough or some sort of connection where a black person or one of another culture such as Hispanic or Spanish was able to be nominated or considered for a job or high-ranking position because someone spoke up for them.

An example of what I am saying regarding a black person being appointed for high-ranking position is when the mayor Fiorello La Guardia appointed Jane Bolin as judge. This came as a surprise to Bolin in 1939; she was not aware of the mayor's intentions, but she made shocking news around the world. My point is it should not have taken almost a century for something like this to happen; thank God for Mayor Fiorello La Guardia's intentions in appointing Jane Boldin as judge.

David L Goodwin seems proud enough to publish in article in the Dutchess County Historical Society yearbook about the first black judge who was Jane Bolin. She was born in Poughkeepsie and had a career in the five boroughs of New York City. This was Jane Matilda Bolin (1908–2007); she is recognized for a particular "first" of the groundbreaking magnitude.

Jane Bolin holds the honor of being the first African American judge in the entire United States joining the bench of New York City's domestic relations score in 1939. Bolin was reappointed by three different mayors: O'Dwyer in 1949, Mayor Wagner in 1959, and Mayor Lindsay in 1969. Bolin's early upbringing in Poughkeepsie was a good one, and she received high marks in school. Although Poughkeepsie was not segregated by the law, Bolin would remember the stares her neighbors gave her and was refuse service at a beauty salon. Bolin also had the experience of being turned down at her neighboring school called Vassar. Vassar did not accept African American students.

In 1924, Bolin was sixteen years old; she became one of two African American freshmen at Wellesley College in Massachusetts. Jane Bolin was also known as the first black woman to graduate from Yale law school and joined the New York City Bar and was the first black to work in the office of the city's corporation counsel. Jane Bolin knew it was difficult for a woman dealing with the law as far as schooling goes, but she believed her case race played a role.

Although she was rejected, she believed in fighting for a good cause even if it humiliated her. She had several quotes. As Jane Bolin said, "As time went by, I was embarrassed by it because it was years after I went on the bench before another African American woman went on the bench." Continued quotes: "I was horrified and transfixed by pictures and news stories of lynchings and other atrocities against blacks solely because of their race." Another one of Jane's quotes: "When I come in, the one or two black probation officers handled only black families, I had that changed."

As Jane Bolin said, "Those gains we have made were never graciously and generously granted. We have had to fight every inch of the way." In addition to Jane's many quotes, "I'm saddened and maddened even nearly half a century later to recall many of my Wellesley experiences, but my college days for that most part evoke sad and lonely personal memories."

She also quoted, "Families and children are so important to our society, and to dedicate your life to trying to improve their lives is completely satisfying." I'd like to elaborate on another one of Jane's quotes: "I wasn't concerned how about first, second, or last. My work was my primary concern."

I have listed several of Jane Bolin's quotes. I'd like to elaborate on the last one mentioned; when Jane emphasized her work being her primary concern, I could strongly relate to Jane's work being her primary concern. My point is it's not what you do, it's how you do it. It's important in life to do whatever it is you do to the best of your ability. In other words, if a person isn't in charge or responsible for a task, then I believe it is imperative that the job is done to the very best of their ability. One must be accountable, especially if the job affects others.

It is critical that people realize their lack of insufficiency can create multiple problems. If people are not responsible or demonstrate proficiency in their work ethic, it's a sign of their inability to get the job done. Jane Bolin not only demonstrated her ability to get the job done, she was a diligent worker. In today's world, it takes dedication, professionalism, willingness, motivation, responsibility, and honesty. After all, one must be true to themselves, especially when the job requires your full attention. This leads to success, respect for yourself, and others. It also shows a caring attitude when a person takes their work seriously.

Jane Bolin was an impeccable worker; she worked for the office of the New York City Corporation. She graced the New York City Bar Association as also being the first African American. Jane worked forty years in the justice system and with an unblemished career. In spite of dealing with all kinds of human behavior, she fought against racial discrimination.

As a judge, Jane Bolin changed the system so publicly funded children were able to be accepted without bias on race or ethnicity. She was a great advocate for children and adults. Jane Bolin was an inspiration to all people regardless of their level of education; she reached out to help others. Jane Bolin asserted herself in a positive way in order for people to know and understand she was an elected official to make a difference in the judicial system.

Jane Bolin falls under the umbrella of many great activists mentioned previously in this book. It's people like Jane

Bolin who give people like me an appreciation for trust in the judiciary system. After all, people must trust and believe that the system will work for them. It is my belief that others feel the same as I do, especially if the system can prove whether or not the person is innocent or guilty; also it takes a person within the right frame of mind, the willingness to be honest and to act in the best interest of whoever is on trial in order to make the right decision after carefully examining the evidence.

Jane Bolin had the qualifications to meet the needs of the people and to serve the people for four decades. It is a fact that it takes a certain caliber of people to humble themselves; it's a realization of the magnitude of the position that they hold. After all, a person's life could be at stake. Jane's continued nominations speaks volumes in her work. It's a clear indication that she had to have been doing something right as well as making a difference as a judge in the judiciary system.

In regard to my research, as I was seeking information, I found supporting literature on Jane Bolin to lend factual support to my writing. Jane Bolin, whom I felt was worthy of making it known to the public that she was a great asset to this country; many people are not aware of the good deeds that people of color have contributed to this country. Jane Bolin was an extraordinary woman who deserved to be mentioned in this book; she devoted her time, skills, and dedication to the public for years.

Bolin worked diligently throughout her lifetime; she was fair and honest while working for the interests of the people. As Bolin performed her duties for the people, she quoted in one of her famous quotes, if it were up to her, she would not retire; she loved her job and performed her occupation well. What Jane Bolin did for the country was an awesome credibility for the judiciary system; she worked hard and maintained her ability to address each case with clarity, accuracy, and factual information.

In my opinion, in reference to Jane Bolin in the above-mentioned, I can attest to the woman of her caliber because evidence supports Jane Bolin's background. In other words, others saw Bolin's ability potential to get the job done, and that's when mayor Fiorello La Guardia appointed Bolin as judge in 1939. This was a huge surprise for Jane and for the people who were able to see the first black female judge be appointed by the mayor in the office at that time. It was a clear indication that someone in a higher position such as the mayor felt that Bolin could do the job. I am more than excited to not only learn about the powerful woman's career in the judiciary system many years ago and to learn about someone so strong and fair-minded having done her job with precision.

Jane Bolin really left a mark in the history books that could be missed if people don't turn the page; it's easy to be forgotten in life, but it's even sadder if you never knew about the person. Therefore, it gives me great pleasure to learn and write about a woman who had such high qualities that she was able to share in the judiciary system years ago. In fact, it's good knowing that a woman was able to get the job done, and an African American woman at that.

Jane Bolin was recognized as the first woman of color in the judiciary system. In addition to Jane Bolin's honorary career, she was reappointed by another mayor, William O'Dwyer, NYC's hundredth mayor, appointed Jane Bolin as judge in 1949. Mayor O'Dwyer had to believe that Jane Bolin was qualified for the job; after all, this was her second term as she was reappointed.

As of this moment I don't know much about Mayor William O'Dwyer, but I can say that he made an excellent choice. Jane Bolin's record speaks for itself, and it clearly depicts her as a person of high standards; the fact that Mayor O'Dwyer even appointed Jane Bolin as judge says something about him. It's obvious that the mayor believed she could continue as judge.

I'd like to add that in life no one never knows who's assessing them or monitoring them to fulfill a position or a need. As I continue to support Jane Bolin's good work over the years, once again Mayor William O'Dwyer confirms my written history regarding Jane Bolin's career; it's publicized that Jane Bolin did an impeccable job as judge. Also, Bolin was once again appointed by a third mayor in 1959; Mayor Robert Ferdinand Wagner appointed her as judge. This was Bolin's third term receiving the appointment as judge. One might say Bolin was a remarkable person who seemed to be liked as well as a suitable candidate. Mayor Wagner had to believe and trust that Jane Bolin was the right person for the job, and in my opinion, I believe that the mayor was able to access Jane's successful years of work as judge, and with that being said, appointing her once again as judge.

I'm sure it is not always easy to appoint someone, especially a black female in New York City. I understand that a mayor's job is not easy, and for him to appoint a woman as judge during an era where women were still fighting for rights, I'm sure he had to see something in Jane Bolin to appoint her. I believe that Mayor Wagner knew of Jane Bolin's credentials and all her achievements as well as her previous years in the judiciary system for him to make a decision to appoint her. This appointment led to Jane Bolin's successful ongoing career as New York City's first female African American judge.

As I continue to share Jane Bolin's history, it's understood that she never allowed anything to come between her doing her job. I know there had to be cases of prejudice that existed during Jane Bolin's appointment while in office; however she remained focused. Even when court cases were racist, Jane still performed her job well. She was a caring person who did not sway her decision or allow herself to be influenced. It is my belief that people hold jobs or professional positions that others see and can tell that they are suited for the job. It shows when a person is elected, appointed, or nominated for a job more than once that they are doing a good job, and I can corroborate that Jane Bolin not only did a good job but that she enjoyed her job as judge.

It's not hard to determine how one feels when it comes to their job; one way or another, a person doesn't have to disclose how they feel about their job. A person's attitude attendance, proficiency, efficiency and being responsible will tell the story about how they value their job. Bolin performed her job well; in fact, it's not hard to see that she was qualified for the position, and she got the job done to the fullest of her ability. In further support in regard to Jane Bolin, I can relate to a woman of her caliber because as I learned about her, I felt more of a connection and was drawn to her after learning so much about her qualities and what she stood for in life and how she helped people.

In addition to my opinion about Jane Bolin, she served the judiciary system with excellence to further elaborate on supporting her as a good judge. In 1969, Mayor John Vliet Lindsey appointed Bolin; it was her fourth appointment. She was appointed by four different mayors at different increments, starting from 1939 to 1969. I see this as no accident. I see this as Jane Bolin's professional character that landed her worthy of these years of appointment as judge.

As she performed her duties, it was noted that over the years she worked hard and proved herself. It is no coincidence that four mayors of different eras in history found it necessary to appoint Jane Bolin. This woman had to have stood for something in their eyes. All four mayors believed in Bolin; they made an excellent choice, and at the same time, she made history by being the first African American judge. As far as I'm concerned, the mayors who appointed Jane Bolin were part of that history too.

CHAPTER 13

Vietnam War

In regard to all the above mentioned on racism, the fight for equal rights during the 1950s through 1970s, the fight was prevalent throughout various states. Black people were fighting for their equal rights; they demanded to be treated like other human beings. Black people were against segregation, homemade laws that consisted of unfair demands that were against their civil rights. As black people fought for many years for their equal rights, there was also another type of fighting going on which was the war that was also known by other names such as the second Indochina War, the American War in Vietnam, the Vietnam conflict of Laos and Cambodia from November 1, 1955 to April 30, 1975, which was second of Indochina War, the Vietnam War, and Nam. This war lasted almost twenty years with the exception of a few months, weeks, and days.

November 1, President Eisenhower deployed the military assistance adversary group to train the army of the Republic of Vietnam. This was the official beginning of the American involvement; more than fifty-eight thousand US troops died. It was the Gulf of Tonkin incident, which was known as the United States Maddox incident, that led to the entry of the United States into Vietnam War. South Vietnam was supported by the United States, along with the other anticommunist allies. North Vietnam was supported by the Soviet Union, China, and other communist allies. The United States was involved in the war for almost twenty years which ceased in 1973. The war is said to be a Cold War involving the United States. The problems spread into neighboring areas such as the Laotian Civil War and the Cambodian War, which resulted in these countries becoming Communist states.

What Caused the Start of the War in Vietnam?

The start of the war in Vietnam stems from North Vietnam and South Vietnam. They were in conflict over a partition into Communist territory. An attempt to prevent communication from taking place was to keep the whole of Southeast Asia and other democracies from becoming a communist region. President John F. Kennedy supported South Vietnam with funding and armaments as well as provided training for the South Vietnam government. This created more conflict between both sides in 1961.

President John F. Kennedy continued funding and offered to send American troops to the region. In 1963, Kennedy was assassinated, but Lyndon B. Johnson continued to follow President John F. Kennedy's work. Johnson deployed twenty-three thousand US soldiers who were drafted during his first year in office. As President, Johnson continued to expand the military aid program because the US made a commitment to send soldiers; thus, more were drafted, which involved more troops eventually being sent to help in the crisis.

According to the statistics over the years, fifty-eight thousand American soldiers were killed. This stirred up the North Vietnamese, and they attacked US naval vessels. The Vietnam War was a long and costly war that angered the communist government of North Vietnam; this led to the fighting. As the war in Vietnam continued, people back home right here in the United States continue to pray for the soldiers' safe return home. People were saddened as they learned about the soldiers being killed. Prayers were constantly being enforced. Many people were occupied with their loved one's friends and families.

Moreover, as the Vietnam War continued, music was played on the radio that I believe helped people get by during these tough times. The soldiers also received musical cassettes from back home that boosted their morale. The radio station played R&B music such as "Bring the Boys Home" by Freda Payne, "What's Going On?" by Marvin Gaye, "Tears of a Clown" by Smokey Robinson and the Miracles, "Sitting on the Dock of the Bay" by Otis Redding, "Green, Green Grass of Home" by Porter Wagoner, "Chain of Fools" by Aretha Franklin, "Mr. Postman" by the Marvelettes, "The Letter" by The Box Tops, "Fortunate Son" by Creedence Clearwater, "Purple Haze" by Jimi Hendrix, "Detroit City" by Bobby Bare, and "I Believe I'm Gonna Make It" by Joe Tex.

These songs and many more were played to comfort family members and the soldiers who were drafted into one of the military branches. The songs during this time had meaning; songs such as "Bring the Boys Home" was constantly hummed with the soldiers in mind with the hope of them returning home, or songs like "Mr. Postman" that provided us with hopes of receiving a letter from a loved one overseas. Also, "What's Going On?" which at the time became an anthem for the nation due to the impact this song had. Gaye was enticed to write this song due to the fact that his brother was in service and in Vietnam at the time.

In 1973, the drafting of soldiers was over. President Richard M. Nixon signed legislation officially ending the draft. It was during this hour of the Vietnam War when soldiers were drafted during peacetime and war until 1973. Nevertheless, as the Vietnam War continued, the music was a big investment that aided the people. The music helped soothe the souls and provided back home long-lasting memories. The music was one thing the soldiers had to hold on to; the music was the thing they could carry into their hearts. I believe the music was the one thing that gave the soldiers hope for returning back home to their friends, family, and spouses. The music was big and popular during the 1960s and 1970s; I believe the lyrics and the beat of the music made it easy for the soldiers and their families to cope with this situation during the Vietnam War.

Moreover, the Vietnam War caused people to be unrelaxed while waiting for their loved ones to return home. It was a time during the Vietnam War where it kept you on your toes due to the unknown. This was not only hard for the families, but it was also harder when families received the news of their loved ones being killed or missing in action. This was devastating news for anyone, friends or family, to receive, when the dog tags came back in place of the bodies or a sealed casket. This was the most terrible news or thing that could happen to anyone.

Also, the soldiers from the Vietnam War had a hard time adjusting to society. Some soldiers needed counseling, support with housing, jobs, and time to readjust to the normal way of society hoping to fit in. The veterans needed support from the Veteran Administration, and this was not always easy. In some instances, veterans were turned down depending on what type of physical or mental need was necessary. The veterans who received physical injuries were given immediate attention whereas if your injury was not visible some of the veterans were not helped at first.

Another problem the veterans faced was being able to care for their families due to the lack of a job or being able to hold a job based on their physical or mental being. I was married to a Vietnam veteran, and I was able to experience the abovementioned. In addition, I had male cousins who came back injured from Vietnam and friends who did not return due to the fact they were dead or missing in action. The condition the soldiers were faced with created a financial hardship for them and their families as well as a big setback. This caused men and women to feel rejected and not appreciated after coming from Vietnam.

There you have it, the Vietnam War was a war that the United States I believe should not have gotten involved in. This war caused many deaths and pain to families who didn't understand why the United States got involved. The Vietnam War created unnecessary loss and hardships throughout the country; we know that the Vietnam War was a long-drawn-out war that was also costly. People back home suffered as well the American soldiers who were fighting in Vietnam. In addition to the United States losing about fifty-eight thousand who were killed, it was also noted that more than half of the dead were Vietnamese citizens. Moreover, the fact in the Vietnam War regarding the deaths of the soldiers were obtained from vietnamwar-history.com.

In 1973, as mentioned previously, President Richard Nixon signed the Paris Peace Accord and ordered the withdrawal of the US forces in 1973. The Vietnam War added stress and anxiety to the American people. This war had people wounded, angry, and fearful that their sons and daughters would not return home. People tried to avoid going into armed forces by dodging the letter by moving from one state to another and even getting a doctor's note that could have kept them from going in the military.

Many people were against the Vietnam War; people felt like Americans had no business in Vietnam fighting a war that didn't concern Americans. People protested the Vietnam War; when veterans returned, many of them never got treated fairly with the respect they deserved. In some instances, the veterans were called baby killers. Nevertheless, the veterans took a lot of abuse, shame, and hurt when they returned from Vietnam. The physical conditions played a painful part in their lives; there are veterans today who still suffer from the Vietnam War. PTSD, Posttraumatic Stress Disorder, which is a health condition that is triggered by something terrifying or something someone experienced.

Many veterans go through sleepless nights talking in their sleep, continuously talking about the war; the veterans tend to hold on to what they experienced during the war. Some show depression, coupled with nervous symptoms. As a wife of a veteran today I can certainly attest to the actions, attitude, and mood swings of a former Vietnam Veteran and a Desert Storm Veteran. Yes, my husband, Willie Goodman, served twice during active duty in Vietnam in 1967 to 1968, finally discharged in 1970 and called back for Desert Storm in 1990 to 1991. He received two honorable discharges after serving two terms; in fact, my husband's military experience has allowed me to empathize with some of the pain and suffering that veterans have experienced.

I've also had the honor of meeting other veterans in my husband's group counseling sessions, and this gave me a clear understanding that other veterans are going through similar symptoms. I've learned over the years how to observe my husband's actions and how to help him cope with his past war experiences. As time moved on, veterans were eventually given the respect and the attention they deserved. There were more supporting services offered like funding, housing restoration, counseling, medical benefits, and much more.

The Veterans' Administration expanded their services for all veterans and offered specific services to meet the needs of the veterans whether it was mortgage discounts or discounts on spending in their local stores like Home Depot or Lowe's department store, just to name a couple. Moreover, the Veterans' Administration offers help for the mentally ill, and they have an emergency number for the veterans to call if they have an emergency or feel suicidal. The Veterans' Administration offers transportation to and from the Veteran hospital; the government has offered through the Veteran Administration opportunity service to aid the men and women who have served this country well. They have helped house veterans who became paralyzed or amputees as a result of the war.

As I talked my way into getting my first apartment, Ninety-Two Morgan Avenue, my husband, Sam, had recently completed his military time. We lived on Morgan Avenue a few years, maintaining the building for the landlady; she seemed to be pleased with what my husband and I were doing and maintaining the building by putting out the garbage, sweeping, and mopping. As a young couple, I believe the landlady was satisfied with the maintenance of the building; we did our best to show her how much we appreciated her giving us a chance to prove to her that we were worthy of a chance to be considered for the apartment, especially since it was an opportunity to demonstrate our independence and to convince our families. We were responsible and mature; the winning advantage was that our parents were close by in case of an emergency.

In lieu of everything that's been said regarding racism and more, allow me to reiterate the Vietnam War between the North and the US, who supported the South, which ended in a victory for the north on April 30 in the year 1975.

This later resulted in the reunification of the country under a communist regime in the upcoming year. Moreover, prior to the Vietnam War, which started in 1954 and ended in 1975, there was another fight going on among the people in the South and the North of the same region or different part of the world. There were people fighting for their rights to be equal and fair treatment to be granted to them as a human being's birthright.

Many activists and strong leaders fought for many years to be given the respect and equal treatment regardless of their color or who they are. In today's world, currently speaking, we still have individuals who choose to divide themselves among various groups. They continue to be biased in the sense of being unfair in the job market, purchasing homes through real estate, in the political arena, and educational field, especially when testing a person's aptitude to determine one's qualifications for certain jobs or positions. Also, price hiking, depending on who the person might be, whether they are buying a home or car for property. There has been price gouging when purchasing property.

An example, I happened to hear about this morning, December 2, 2022, on channel 7 news involved two women: a black woman, you know, Caucasian woman decided to change houses temporarily. The Austins' house was appraised for just $1,000,000 more then what they originally said despite spending $400,000 in cost. They received a slap in the face. The Austins asked one of their Caucasian friends to pose as though the house belonged to her. The house appraised $1,482,000, or about $500,000 more for the Caucasian family. This change was said to be almost a 50 percent increase in volume; it is a known fact that blacks are rejected for mortgage loans at rates triple times higher than that of white applicants.

If the Caucasian woman did not pretend to be Tanisha, who decided to bring over photos of her and her family who are white and made the black family home look like it belonged to the Caucasian family. The Austins' were outraged and angry; this has caused or led to the black family's low rates when it came to owning their own home. It is clear that "we know discrimination is in nearly every aspect of that home buying process," said Jessica Lautz, National Association of Realtors vice president of demographics and behavioral insights. "We need to be addressing it as an industry."

Another example of bias my, husband then and I experienced was when we decided to purchase our first home. I was twenty years old in the year 1971; I was too young to recognize what was really going on when the realtor showed a house in Queens. As the realtor parked his car, we did the same and parked as well. Once we approached a particular house with the realtor, the neighborhood was clear of all people. We went into the home that was being shown by the realtor; again the neighborhood was clear of all people.

When my husband and I came out of the house, most of the neighbors were suddenly standing on their porch. I felt a little uneasy. I didn't quite understand what was happening, but I know now I can remember it like it was yesterday, and I can see clearly now the people were looking and wondering if we were going to purchase that house.

It saddens me to see that some people are determined to cheat, mistreat, or believe that certain individuals have no rights unless they are of a certain ethnic origin. I believe it's the negative attitude of the people coupled with their upbringing. If children are trained early to appreciate the differences in the people of the world, this could be a better place for all mankind. The gift of life represents God's love; if we say we love the world or the people in the world, love is what you do; therefore, mistreating others who are not like you is a sign of prejudice against people of different backgrounds.

I recall when my second husband and I purchased the house we are living in today in 2015, we also had a similar problem. The broker had to tell his boss that we were his family. The broker claimed that my husband was his wife's uncle in order to help get us approved for the purchasing of the property. We never asked why the broker had to use that approach to get us approved for the property. I wasn't sure why, and I never asked or thought twice about it; I know my husband and I were both working citizens, which he was retired after twenty-five years from the Transit Authority, and I was approaching my retirement for the New York City Board of Education as a teacher of thirty-one years.

In addition to the abovementioned examples of prejudice in housing, there is also bias in the Police Department, school system, and courthouse. As we hear the news daily a lot, there have been reports of more blacks being stopped or pulled more frequently than Caucasians. My husband and I were pulled over a few times by the police.

I remember one incident where the police thought we didn't stop at a stop sign on Hook Creek Ave in Queens; the officer then questioned us asking where we are coming from. When we responded telling him we were coming from church in Brooklyn, he wanted to know if we lived in Long Island why are we coming or attending a church in Brooklyn. My response to the officer was it's my family's church. It was the car in front of us that failed to stop. Once we explained this to the police, he should have accepted the explanation; the officer should have avoided ongoing questions like where and why.

In terms of the school system, teachers are denied promotions depending on who they are and what position they are seeking. I received a position appointed by a black administrator, and several Caucasian women asked me who do I think I am, and I told them back then I was a different person than what I am today. Today I learned how to deflect prejudice and biased situations in a different way. I approach all people with love, a warm greeting, a smile coupled with kindness. I realized what I was up against on my job, and I could not let ignorant people turn me into what I was not raised to be, as I know love and I came from a family of love. One might say, what's love got to do with it? Everything! Love is what you do; love is the key to help bring about change.

People must realize who they are and understand God's principles as well as God's gift to all mankind. I strongly believe we have a purpose in life; the purpose could involve doing a kind act, helping someone, recognizing a need. If people could demonstrate sharing and caring about other people, I believe this could make a difference in our world today.

In addition, the courthouse cases having been determined based on who you are. It seems that blacks and minorities might receive stricter punishments as opposed to Caucasians, according to a journal article on differential punishing of African Americans and whites who possess drugs.

Policies should be adjusted or a continuation of the past, where blacks were charged with twenty years of incarceration. It seems that 97 percent of blacks are arrested for cocaine and 80 percent of people arrested for cocaine powder were white. It was contested by five African American constitutionality of the statute. After the courts upheld the challenge, they ruled the statute unconstitutional. This took place in the Minnesota Supreme Court (*state vs. Russell*, 1991).

There was an issue of whether African Americans are punished more severely than a white American by the criminal justice system and whether the system is racist has been debated in the literature (Blumstein, 1982; Johnson, 1992, Peter and Hagan, 1984). Some criminal justice professionals called the black studies, vol. 28 no. 1, September 1997, 97–11, 1997, Sage Publication Inc.

Loudmouth

There were many well-known leaders in America's civil rights movement. There were thousands of marchers fighting to build a better society, Al Sharpton, along with many others. For a long time, he is one of the greatest activists of the twentieth century right into the twenty-first century. Sharpton worked with many who fought for equal rights of others, primarily for black people who have never been treated fairly in many instances. For instance, Claudette Calvin and three of her friends were sitting on the bus, and the driver asked her to move to the back. The three ladies moved, but Claudette didn't, and she went to jail because she refused to listen to the driver, who insisted that they all move to the back of the bus just because a white woman boarded the bus. We know today Rosa Parks was known for refusing to give up her seat, but it was Claudette Calvin who returned nine months later.

Al Sharpton worked diligently to get people to see and understand that people should be treated with respect, dignity, and, equality regardless of who they are. He was one of the late Dr. Martin Luther King Jr's. close advisers. Al Sharpton played a role in the 1963 March on Washington advocating for jobs and freedom to assist King's memoir, which was an approach toward freedom.

As we understand, the equal rights movement was also important for the entire world; the civil rights movement was an approach to segregation and discrimination. It was one of the main reasons why people fought to bring about change. As time went on, the movement finally put a stop toward segregation legally and publicly, and this completely redesigned America's social system, which was a process.

The civil rights movement was to protect people and to ensure that their equal rights were not denied because of their color or ethnicity. This movement was formed to protect minority groups like Hispanics, African Americans, women, and up until recently lesbian, gay, bisexual, and transgender as well. There are several amendments—thirteenth, fourteenth, fifteenth, nineteenth, and twenty-sixth—pertaining to the Constitution. Although race today is still or can be a problem, it is important that people examine themselves to help identify the core of the problem.

It is my belief that people must become aware of who they are and analyze what they can do to continue the process of what racial equality means. In all fairness, everybody should be treated equally; for instance, when seeking housing, employment, schools, and anything that is in the best interest of the people equal rights are not, not just for certain groups who feel they have the right to control minorities or people who are not like them. It is my belief that all people must understand and have an awareness of the things in life and realize the God-given gift that entitles all human beings a fair and equal opportunity in life.

This world is temporary housing for us. We came with nothing, and we leave this world with nothing. Therefore, people are not focused on their actions and their beliefs as well as their attitude toward other people. It's important that people value life and truly understand its imperative that they respect other people regardless of their color or ethnicity. I trust that if people are trained early on in their upbringing this can make a difference on how people think, act, and feel toward people who are not like them. This is no guarantee, but early training can make a difference. In all that's been said with regard to respect for people of all races, there is the responsibility of individuals to acknowledge their actions whether negative or positive.

Moreover, let me introduce Al Sharpton who was occasionally called Loudmouth Al Sharpton. Sharpton was mentioned early on in the writing, but he had a certain method in attempting to get the attention of the people; he didn't get the "Loudmouth Al Sharpton" title for nothing. His approach was loud enough to get the attention of the public. He knew the people didn't want to hear anything about the civil rights.

Sharpton fought for decades trying to get fair treatment for the people; he dealt with police for years; he was the head of the National Youth Movement in the eighties. Al Sharpton Formed mini marches trying to get people to realize their wrongdoings toward people of color as he was trying to address the rest of the issues people did not want to hear it. It is my thinking that those people who were yelling, "Go home!" were the problem, as Sharpton excited the people who supported him invoicing concerns. There was still much control throughout the nation.

CHAPTER 14

Loudmouth Al Sharpton

In regard to Reverend Al Sharpton, he was one of Dr. Martin Luther King Jr's. strongest advocates before King died on April 4, 1968. Al Sharpton worked hard, along with other activists as previously mentioned. He sacrificed much time and effort over the years trying to get people to do all the right things according to the law and the rights of the people.

Al created the National Youth Movement in the 1980s. Al had a strategy to get the attention of the people because he was not invited to address the public, so he used his strategy, which is how he got the name Loudmouth. Al Sharpton fought for decades to control his story because the media stated that he was confrontational and divisive or demonstrating hostility toward people. Al's focus was to fight to control this story as he felt people needed to know the truth.

Al fought to change some of the laws and to address racism. He formed marches so that people can understand his purpose as well as realize what he was about. I believe people cannot change the minds of people. Al knew that certain laws could make a difference in terms of the people having equal rights. Al emphasized why he was doing what he did; he worked to address the civil rights of the people and felt a need to address issues that were unjust toward African Americans. He was trying to get people to lay aside their differences in order to make the nation whole.

Al was concerned with the three black boys who had an incident in 1986, which involved Michael Griffith. He knew that racism existed in Howard Beach; Michael was killed December 20, 1986, in Howard Beach, Queens, New York, in a racially motivated attack. As the people learned about this attack, Al Sharpton fought for change in the law; he and other activists' goal was to make sure those responsible for the death of Michael Griffith be punished.

Al Sharpton continued to get the attention of the people. He formed marches for the rights of the laws to be implemented and executed; he was about legislative change because the criminal justice system was not meeting the needs of black people. Al thought if changing the laws to meet the needs of the people it could help change society. There was death after death where blacks were being mistreated or killed.

Al Sharpton fought decades for black people to be treated fair; it seems as though he was not being heard and people were deliberately ignoring the concerns of the people purposely. Moreover, there had been multiple police killings: Yusuf Hawkins, August 23, 1989; Sean Bell, November 25, 2006; Trayvon Martin, February 26, 2012; Eric Garner, July 17, 2014; Breonna Taylor, March 13, 2020; and George Floyd, May 25, 2020.

As a result of the tragic killings, Al Sharpton and others felt a need to try and get justice for the families and friends of the victims. This is a few of the unjust killings. As Al continued to seek justice, on April 2021, Officer Derek Chauvin, forty-six years old, finally was charged manslaughter. On February 25, 2022, three other officers—J. Alexander Kueng, Thomas Lane, and Tou Thao—were found guilty of the deprivation of Floyd's civil rights. This unfair treatment toward blacks went on too long. I know as a human being people are entitled to a fair hearing; the law says a person is innocent until proven guilty. This should apply to all people; in many cases, it does not. If a person mistreats an animal, they are breaking the law; if a person is mistreated the perpetrator, they don't seem to acknowledge the unlawful act that they are doing to the victim.

In reference to all Al Sharpton believed, he was misunderstood in more ways than one. As I said, people did not want to hear what Sharpton had to say. I can relate to Sharpton using the approach he did because he found it was necessary to use a loud approach to get people to hear what he had to say. In my opinion, sometimes this does not always work; it is my belief that Sharpton wanted to desperately help people. I know and believe people cannot change, especially if they are set in their ways and their mind is made up.

There was more to just helping people obtain equal rights for everyone, and to eliminate double standards for certain ethnic groups, Sharpton felt that if laws could be put in place this could help as opposed to certain groups of people being ignored or taken advantage of. Al Sharpton's loudmouth approach, I believe, helped him in so many ways, but it hurt him as well. Sharpton's loudmouth approach helped him release his frustration and at the same time caused him to be arrested for what he thought was wrong, especially since he was trying to be understood. In terms of Al Sharpton's approach, many people we know did not approve of his loud approach, and I believe this hindered him in so many ways. People were shouting as he tried to speak; the crowd was cursing and shouting offensive words and yelling obscene language, using the N word. Despite all this, Al Sharpton continued to protest, give speeches, and organize marches. He worked hard over the years, and to this present day, I understand how Al Sharpton wanted to help people of color.

He fought for years to change some of the laws. Many people were treated unfairly; as of today, some of that long, hard fighting paid off. As we take a closer look into the laws and society, we see Al Sharpton and other activists changed some laws and attitudes of the people. Sharpton was protesting for all people to receive equal rights. Sharpton believed that everyone, not just some people, should have a right to be treated fairly, whether they are black or white.

Al Sharpton worked with Dr. Martin Luther King Jr. to promote civil rights regardless of race, religion, ethnicity, and whether you were a male or female; in other words, Sharpton's belief was affiliated with Dr. Martin Luther King Jr's views. Al Sharpton was born on October 3, 1954; in addition to him being an American civil rights activist he is a Baptist minister, a talk show host, and politician.

In 2004, Al Sharpton was a candidate for the presidential nomination; he also ran many other times for different offices. In 1992 he ran for US Senate, and in 1994, he also ran for New York City mayor's office. In 1997 Al Sharpton held the title as a leading civil rights activist. He is the founder of the National Action Network (NAN). He started this organization in 1991; his focus is to continue the legacy of Dr. Martin Luther King Jr. His goal is to fight for social justice for all Americans.

Today, Al Sharpton continues to work hard serving the people and addressing issues in various communities that need to be addressed or questioned; he has worked hard over the years, emphasizing the needs of the people, especially those who are less fortunate and need assistance. I learned over the years that Al Sharpton sacrificed his time and energy trying to change laws to help bridge people together; in my opinion, this was Al Sharpton's main goal.

Sharpton used a loudmouth approach to be heard. Many people might not have agreed with his approach; I believe Sharpton did what he thought was best at the time. He knew people did not want to hear what he had to say; it is my belief that sometimes you must step out of your comfort zone. As we know, you can't please some of the people all the time. I believe if people were willing to face the truth Al Sharpton's loudmouth approach might not have been used in today's world. People tend to forget about reoccurring situations or incidents in society as long as it does not affect them or their family.

It is a fact that life is too short to ignore what's going on around you; if people had a chance to help someone that's not like them, would they do it for money or from the heart? As the question popped into my mind, I'm proud to say having a heart and the love for all people really makes a difference because money can't replace love. We the people must open our hearts to others as well as our eyes; it is imperative that people recognize others who tried to do a good deed to help people as opposed to turning the other cheek.

Al Sharpton became involved in life to help change wrongful situations. I hope and believe it won't take a lifetime to see that racism, bias, and prejudice against people is not worth it. I believe it takes a certain caliber of people to try to make a difference in the world. As an activist, I believe we need more people in today's world like Al Sharpton and other activists of the past. Moreover, racism cannot thrive unless we allow it; if people could focus on their mindset and not what was told or taught to them regarding racism, I strongly believe we would be closer to change in terms of respecting others and realizing that beauty lies in the hearts of people regardless of their ethnicity.

In my writing, I hope something is said that will allow you to reflect on life and see the value of its purpose. It is my hope that the information in this book can be shared with others and also viewed as resourceful and an inspiration to the people. I want to say regardless of who fights for the rights of the people it's right to fight if something is worthy of a fight, especially if the problem affects multiple backgrounds of people in a prejudiced demeanor.

It would be unfair not to stand up for equal rights that all human beings are entitled to if an injustice were the case; it's more than right to protect people when they can't protect or fight for themselves. Human beings have rights, and they deserve to be treated in accordance to the law, which is supposed to enforce by the imposition of penalties. However, this is not always implemented, and this is one of the many reasons people try to get the law to represent them as well as protect them.

CHAPTER 15

The Adult Awakening in Life's Reality

As time passed and I became more involved in society, I realized the world was not fair to people. I witnessed social injustices, inequality within the workplace, and so much more. The common denominator for each of these incidents is tied to discrimination or prejudice.

As an adult, I know I had to face reality with not just understanding who I am but with taking a stand; the safety net that I once knew was no longer in existence. As an adult, I didn't have what I grew up with; a new life had taken a turn and my perceptions as a child growing up with a mixed race of people changed. I had the experience of multicultural people of various backgrounds. While growing up I learned all about loving people for who they were regardless of color or one's nationality. I felt love in my neighborhood. I felt safe; most of all I was able to see that people can get along even if they are different due to their culture or heritage. I had the experience of being exposed to multicultural people, allowing me as a person to have a greater love for all mankind. I am a lover of all people; my upbringing and background played a major role in who I am today. I was taught love growing up; I learned about respect for people early in life no matter what race or color. Exposure to a lifestyle you never experienced before can help eliminate stereotypes.

Once I left my environment, I experienced racism and hate in other communities. There was a time when my cousins and I were chased back to our neighborhood and called names. We ran from the school, JHS 111, in Brooklyn all the way home. I knew people were taught to hate people who are not like them. My cousins and I were able to experience love at home in our neighborhood and hate outside of our environment. On the other hand, as an independent adult, it became clear that I had to work hard, show, and prove who I am. I no longer had the safe environment I could run to. I had to take a stand in life by showing people that black people can be successful educators and business owners, just like white people.

As an adult, I have encountered racism, but as an independent, strong black woman, I am not intimidated when I feel unwelcomed or denied the right to something or a position. I have learned to pursue the situation, and I have learned to never give up, especially if I have earned the right to whatever it is I am seeking. In my writing, I previously mentioned how I convinced the white landlord to rent me my first apartment at the age of eighteen. The lady outright told me she didn't want to rent to blacks, but I was able to convince her to rent to my husband and me. We kept the building clean, set out the garbage, and made a lasting impression to the lady.

As an adult in the workplace, I worked in the private sector. I worked hard and could never get a promotion or a particular day off. I watched new people get days off and receive promotions. I did get a lot of promises regarding a promotion, but it never happened. I was qualified and never had an unsatisfactory work review; however, due to the color of my skin, I was overlooked. I left the job because I refused to continue with false promises; I knew I deserved better, so I left the company.

The reality of this scenario was that the company was prejudiced. They rewarded who they deemed worthy depending on what the color of your skin was, as opposed to one's qualifications. In addition, there were more jobs where people were not fair, but once you realize this, you continue to do your best and wait for an opportunity to be accepted based on your merit. I recall during my career as a teacher I applied for a promotion that I knew I was qualified for and met the job standards, but hateful, prejudiced people apparently felt differently. I was qualified, and I had every right to elevate myself, but once again, it seemed to boil down to who you were at the time.

I can truly say that knowing who I am and having a beautiful upbringing consisting of love and people of many races helped mold my character, personality, and my whole demeanor. My negative experiences did not cause me to hate people who displayed hate. The negative racist encounters made me stronger; in fact, they taught me to not only love harder but to love more and do more in terms of teaching others to love and respect human beings regardless of one's heritage.

In today's world, we as black people still have a long way to go to be accepted in some instances. We have come a long way, but we are still not there. Many people don't realize the beauty in accepting people for who they are and respecting those who are not like them. There were and still are many people who fought for equal rights in respect for all human beings. People must realize we are here on borrowed time and having hate is not worth it and being prejudiced is not God's way. In fact, I believe God had nothing but love for the people.

Nevertheless, the love that I received growing up has not only sustained me but has made a difference in my life and taught me to do unto others as you would like them to do unto you. This is what love has done for me. People must wake up and realize you're here today and could be gone today. It's obvious people can be selfish, rude, and conceited to the point where they're not going to change their ways toward other people. I've realized hate exists on both sides; black people have displayed hate toward white people as well.

Many times, you may have seen or heard a black person show prejudiced acts toward white people as well. I believe blacks have become angry in some cases by the way they have been treated over the years by white people. There was a time when black people were beat by the police during the late fifties and sixties. There was a time when the police turned the dogs loose and water hoses on black people in the South. This created hate toward white people.

I believe black people became angry over the years when they could see or hear about how blacks were being treated in the South. This knowledge about the treatment blacks were getting caused them pain and anger toward white people. It doesn't make it right for black people to retaliate with hate and prejudiced acts because of the past; many people should know that racism is something that can be hurtful and cause one to be resentful, angry, and hostile toward those who have a problem with people who are not like them.

As a consequence, I believe black people behaved in such a way according to what they experienced over the years in terms of disrespect to the black race. Also, in the past, blacks have been made to feel inferior to the white people. If people are denied, rejected, or not given an opportunity to prove themselves, it does not mean they are inferior or incapable. It simply means white people are heartless, selfish, mean, and conceited to the point that they believe they've done nothing wrong in the past toward blacks and other minority groups. It's important for my story to be told because had it not been for my family, I don't know what or where I would be today in this world.

I met my great-grandmother, who was born in 1871 and died in 1982. She was alive during a pivotal time in history when blacks experienced the worst of the racism. This woman, Annie Minter, gave me my strength, as well as my parents. I met her in 1981 at her son's funeral who died at the age of eighty-eight. My great-grandmother gave me the strength and drive to be strong, after all she had experienced during her lifetime.

Moreover, I'd like to say it seems people are capable of coming together when there is a real tragedy in this world. People tend to connect by showing a concern for others by taking and supporting one another. For instance, on September 11, 2001, the World Trade Center was bombed. When this occurred, people were working together to help each other. It didn't seem to matter if you were black or white, people joined in to help save lives of those who were trapped or in danger of losing their lives. People seem to reach out to help those in need of jobs, money, housing, and family who lost their loved ones. I recall a sixth-grade student in my school down the hall from my class lost her mom that morning. It was a sad day, but I remember the teachers donating money and clothes to the family.

Once again, people came together during the pandemic in 2020 to assist each other. It was obvious that people united to help save those who were sick or trying to avoid others from getting sick by encouraging them to wear masks and to distance themselves from the sick. In the medical field, doctors and nurses worked overtime to save people; it didn't matter what your ethnicity was; at least it didn't seem to when it came to saving a life during the pandemic. People were helping others willingly. People reached out to communicate their concerns regarding COVID-19. They were informing you on where to get tested or treatment. There were many people offering advice on how to stay safe; it was apparent that you could feel the concern and love that was shared by all people. It was a time when people were definitely afraid of dying; people were in fear for their lives and their families' lives.

It was evident that people bonded together to try to make sense out of what was going on with so many people dying due to COVID-19 and other variants. My final point is, does it take a drastic tragedy or a serious crisis to bring people together? It seems like people refused to recognize that humanity should prevail over ignorance, disrespect, and prejudice toward mankind.

CHAPTER 16

Book Closing

In my attempt to finalize my writing, it gives me great pleasure to share my life story on how I was raised by my parents, aunts, and uncles. It was a time where everyone got involved in raising and protecting children.

As I mentioned early on in the book, I and my siblings were fortunate to have multiple relatives living in the same area of Williamsburg, Brooklyn, on Morgan Avenue. I believe family, love, and support help to make a difference in one's life. The family input can determine an individual's adulthood well-being. Family support and love can contribute to a person's success in life.

I felt a strong need to share my story simply because I was raised in a family where all we had was laughter, love, and each other, along with jokes. I am living proof that a person or people can be successful growing up with a lack of money in their household. Respect and love are what sustained us and kept us doing the right thing. Therefore, the lack of money can still mean success for people; like the Beatles said in March of 1964 in their song, I know money can make a difference in one's lifestyle, but it can't always make one happy.

I believe family involvement in many cases can make a difference in the lives of people. It's important to have a system that supports you, along with a value system to help influence one's life. I believe family support can outweigh the lack of money. Having a balanced lifestyle can help people understand their purpose in life. It's important for people to realize a strong family can grow together and be a help to each other. I am a product of the abovementioned in regard to family, love, and support.

However, where people lack the love and support of a family, it is my belief that they can allow another person to act as a surrogate parent to help them have a lifestyle that can help them grow into a well-balanced person who can allow them to have a successful life as well. Moreover, my reason for telling my story is to let the reader know it's important to show love to others and to understand that life consists of hatred in all types of prejudices. It's imperative that love is displayed in a family's home early on in life and that children are taught to share and love others.

I strongly believe racism starts early in the young minds of children. As I grew up, much love was shared in my life; that's why I believe if people are willing to teach children the importance of loving others as opposed to demonstrating hate for other people this world can be a better place to live in. As much as it is hard to pinpoint the start of racism, it's easy to recognize and feel other people's prejudices and them being a racist. If people are unfortunate to not have a loving life growing up, they still can learn how not to be prejudiced toward others. As I explained, people must realize that all human beings need to be treated with dignity and respect for all mankind.

The point I'm trying to make is that whether children are raised by their biological family members or surrogate members, it is vital that love plays a role in the lives of the children. People can make a big difference when teaching others to show love as opposed to hate. It had been years where people had been dealing with hatred and racism. Many people have fought throughout the world for equality for all people. This has been an ongoing problem for decades and still is in today's world.

As I mentioned in my book title, racism only thrives if we allow it in today's world; racism still exists throughout. People are being clandestine about the reality of racism. I want to close by saying people have a lot in common. As human beings I can only wonder what the problem is when it comes to respecting people who are not like them. The fact that people are human should be enough of a reason to show love toward each other and avoid bias or prejudice to be inserted in situations.

If people are learning about hate at an early age, teaching hate, supporting hate, encouraging hate, being about hate, it doesn't go away. The fight for equal justice has gone on too long. When does it stop? We are on borrowed time living the gift of life. Where will we be if God was prejudiced or treated certain people differently? What would the world look like if a higher power were racist?

All human beings should be treated with respect; what if the tables were turned? In other words, how would you feel if people were hating you, denying you of an opportunity to advance or prosper in life? No one wants to be put in a position where they are made to feel less than human.

As I expressed my feelings, I hope the reader can relate to all that I am addressing. I hope you can feel the love in your hearts as opposed to the lack of love that people have been subjected to over decades of disrespect. There have been many years of mistreatment to people who are not like those who are doing the mistreatment to various groups of people. It is time for change in the world. I know it is easier said than done; people can make change if they really want to, not if they are pressured to. It should come from the heart.

In other words, looking back over the years on how people were treated and how blacks had to fight for what they believed in is enough to make you want to see a change in people. Many people have endured long, hard suffering as a result of fighting for equal rights.

In closing, I'd like to say I am grateful that my heart is filled with love for people of all ethnic backgrounds. I am proud to want to help people no matter their color or background. It is important to me to share my love and hope that someone who reads my story might be given a different perspective on life and the clear understanding of their purpose on the planet. The mistreatment of certain groups of people over history had gone on too long; time is of the essence. We cannot get back what should have never happened, but we can move forward and talk about good deeds of kindness. We can help others by talking to them if they need assistance as opposed to hating or encouraging others to hate.

We the people can offer advice, seek information, and give them ideas that can help with a need. It doesn't take much to be kind and helpful to others. I believe it's not about us; it's all about being a blessing toward others. I say yes to the people; we can move forward. There was always room for going ahead in life. If people can understand that love is the answer to help the people of the world and be willing to change their ways if need be, it would be a better world. If people could look in the mirror, see themselves and realize they too can be a leading example to possibly make a difference in the world by simply showing love, compassion, and concern for others, especially those who don't look like them.

I recall a few days ago I was leaving McDonald's, and prior to my leaving, a woman and I made eye contact; we smiled at each other for a minute. On my way out, I shook her hand and then placed the dollar bill in her hand; the woman was overwhelmed. She could not believe my actions toward her.

This kind act was a spontaneous one. It's important to be a blessing to others. In today's times people are hurting; they are lacking so much. This is just one monetary example of being kind to people. I believe doing an unjust act to others or people not like you will get you nowhere. We the people can make the world a better place by realizing it's up to the people.

It is a process for people to change. I know and understand nothing happens overnight, but I can say it's like finding a needle in the haystack. However, I'm not discouraged; in fact, I'm inspired to be able to express my feelings and love for people. It's like having a heart full of candy, sharing it and spreading the love as far as it will go to all mankind.

CHAPTER 17

Wall of Fame

A wall of a few activists who played a part in the fight for equal justice for all and those who told their stories:

    Martin Luther King Jr.
    Rosa Parks
    John Lewis
    Adam Clayton Power
    Ralph David Abernathy
    Andrew Young
    Nelson Mandela
    Arthur Ashe
    Jane Bolin
    Annette Gordon-Reed
    Bill Russell
    Al Sharpton

ABOUT THE AUTHOR

Author Doris Goodman is known for her many good deeds in society throughout her lifetime. She has touched many hearts and helped to empower people at work, church, and in her community. She has the ability to influence individuals, encouraging them to enhance themselves to their fullest potential. She has a positive, strong drive when recommending people to be exigent toward their goals to be successful.

It is her belief that everyone can produce a lifestyle that can promote an intellectual level of education. She also believes that exigence for an education positively can contribute toward a person's outcome in life and help determine whether or not they prevail throughout life.

Doris Goodman believes that life is designed to bring about change and people must be mindful and prepared to act in such a way with regard to the situation in order to comply with the necessary circumstances. She sees life as being a challenge or possibly a test. It is her belief that no one has to fail or should fail in all their endeavors, providing that individuals work diligently toward achieving their goals.

Doris Goodman believes that motivation plays a major role in ones success. She believes that anyone motivated in life can have success. People can be motivated in their jobs or school, provided they have a strong drive for what they want to achieve in life. Doris Goodman strongly respects the value of learning and the power to fight to build one's ability to bring about change.

Doris Goodman's belief is that nothing can happen in life if people don't initiate a plan of action that can lead to ones success. It is imperative that people strive to be all that they can be in order to live in a way that is rewarding and gives them the opportunity to be successful in all their endeavors. Doris Goodman strongly believes that life is designed to allow people to appreciate living and understand the values and purpose of being on earth. She understands that people can be whatever they choose to be, provided they are willing to work hard and obtain their interests and goals in order to get the most out of life.

Moreover, Doris Goodman is convinced that people understand that the choices they make in life can determine a positive outcome for how well they can fulfill their dreams and goals. It is a fact that time is of the essence, and the mind is a terrible thing to waste. Among the many challenges in life, there is hope, and with hope, one can achieve whatever one desires.

In addition, Doris Goodman is confident that all things are possible for people to excel in life, provided that people take advantage of resources, technology, and support from others with the same interests and experiences. It does not take much to inquire about how to seek assistance that can help one improve their quality of life.

In summary, Doris Goodman's assumptions state that it is people's choices what they want out of life.

Printed in the USA
CPSIA information can be obtained
at www.ICGtesting.com
CBHW040108301024
16599CB00061B/982